RESEARCH GUIDE IN
history

RESEARCH GUIDE IN
history

John R. M. Wilson
Minot State College

Consulting Editor: Carl Kalvelage

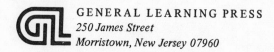

GENERAL LEARNING PRESS
250 James Street
Morristown, New Jersey 07960

Preface

It is more important to learn the techniques of finding, interpreting, and relating historical information than it is to
memorize or learn historical data. According to psychologists,
we forget over 90 percent of the facts we learn in college within
five years of graduation. By writing term papers, essays, and
theses in history, the student acquires the technique of gather-
ing information and perspective on the human condition. My
goal is to aid the student in gaining such skills.

This research guide, designed for the history student,
directs him to resource material and explains how to organize
and document a research paper. The text offers hints about
finding topic ideas in the library and provides assistance in
formulating a hypothesis and drawing up an outline. It includes
a number of features to which most students are not generally
exposed, including a ranking of graduate history departments,
brief sketches of top historians, and an annotated list of important historical journals.

The source list does not pretend to be exhaustive at the
graduate level, but it does list the main source materials with
which the history student should be familiar. I believe that the
student will find this guide adequate for even the most demand-
ing research paper in the area of history. I regret that there was
no such guide in my own undergraduate days.

I wish to thank Kenneth D. Roose, Charles J. Anderson,
and the American Council on Education for permission to use
material from *A Rating of Graduate Programs.* In addition, for

sections taken from the *Research Guide for Undergraduates in Political Science,* I owe a debt to Carl Kalvelage, Morley Segal, and Peter J. Anderson. The Macmillan Company has graciously approved inclusion of material from *Paths to the Present* by Arthur M. Schlesinger, Sr. William Tanner offered valuable comments, criticisms, and suggestions that contributed to the final text. Most of all, I wish to thank my wife Mary for the tremendous assistance she has provided in preparing this book, help which went beyond the usual secretarial and morale areas into the realm of research.

John R. M. Wilson

Contents

Part I

HOW TO RESEARCH AND WRITE A PAPER IN HISTORY

Researching and Writing a Paper in History

The research paper is one of the basic tools of scholarship. It is the written result of careful investigation of a chosen topic and is intended to display simultaneously the student's grasp of the topic and his ability to express himself in a scholarly fashion.

The completion of a research paper to the instructor's satisfaction indicates a *tour de force* by the student that transcends the rote of simple recall and is a badge assuring some expertise in the chosen subject. The instructor may also be assured that his student has learned where and how to search out information; how to use the library; how to take accurate notes; how to support ideas with footnotes; how to list a bibliography so that others may turn to cited sources; and most important, how to organize his thoughts on a given topic.

In history, as in every discipline, the research paper is a scholar's credentials—credentials that must be earned. And to this end the following suggestions are offered as aids to choosing, researching, and writing a topic in history.

UNDERSTANDING THE TOPIC

If the instructor should assign a topic, the student's first step clearly must be to familiarize himself with that topic. This endeavor should lead him to the relevant pages of the class text, to some other introductory text, or to a general or subject encyclopedia, handbook, glossary, etc.

If, on the other hand, the choice of topic is left to the student (the rule in college rather than the exception), he must be prepared for an intellectual struggle. For selecting an initial topic can be a time-consuming and frustrating task. An entire section (pp. 13-18), therefore, has been devoted to helping the individual choose an interesting and manageable topic.

OUTLINING THE PROJECT

Working from the supposition that a topic has already been selected, the next step is to make a statement of purpose, revealing as precisely as possible the intention of the writer. Where does he plan to direct his topic? How does he plan to treat it generally? With what approach and to what end? Each word of this statement should be scrutinized for exact meaning.

Then, on the basis of a preliminary survey of the topic, a rough outline is prepared, an outline that is divided into as many chapters and subchapters as possible. Here, for the first time, the various angles of the topic to be investigated are listed. And it is this incipient outline that will be the student's constant guide for research—constant, but never unalterable. An outline is a skeleton, rather, of the final report, to which may be added or from which may be deleted material for the final draft. There are several strong reasons for constructing this outline (none of which is the didactic whim of the instructor), but the strongest is that it gives direction to all subsequent research.

PREPARING A BIBLIOGRAPHY

The best point of departure in preparing a bibliography is the bibliography in the class text, using those titles that appear to deal directly with the assigned or selected topic. Next, the student simply checks the library to see if those books or journals or pamphlets are in stock; this is most easily done by examining the card catalog files kept by all libraries—alphabetized by authors, titles, and subjects, with all books listed in each.

The periodicals can be covered through the indexes and abstracts that are kept scrupulously up-to-date by librarians. The index lists information such as where and when the article was published, while the abstract gives this information plus a brief résumé of the article's contents. References such as these are arranged by author, title, subject, or even a combination of all these. Examples include *Reader's Guide to Periodical Literature* (p. 73), *The New York Times Index* (p. 73), *Social Sciences and Humanities Index* (p. 74), *Historical Abstracts, 1775-1945* (p. 71), and *America: History and Life* (p. 69). These sources, since they refer to journals and magazine articles rather than published book-length treatments, are the sources of the freshest material.

The best and easiest way to prepare a bibliography is to use 4 X 6 or 5 X 8 index cards, lined or unlined, on which to note the pertinent data. Across the top of these cards is written the name of the author, title of the book, the edition, place of publication, publisher, date of publication, and volume number.

If the material is contained in a journal, the necessary data include the author, title of the article, name of the journal, volume number, date of publication, and the page numbers covering the article. In either case, the library classification number should be added. A separate card, of course, should be used for each entry.

CHECKING THE BIBLIOGRAPHY

Once the bibliography is compiled, it becomes urgent to determine if the volumes and journals listed are, indeed, available in the library. And if they are, then the student must scan them to be certain that they contain material relevant to the topic.

Using the library classification numbers, the student can go directly to the shelf where a check of the chapter contents or the index of a volume will determine if it can be of use. If this proves positive, then a notation on the index card should explain in what way it can be used.

USING THE LIBRARY CARD CATALOG

Practically every library in the United States uses one of two classification systems—the Dewey decimal classification or the Library of Congress classification. These two classification systems differ in their approach; an explanation of each follows.

Dewey Decimal Classification

Melvil Dewey worked out this approach in the latter part of the nineteenth century. The Dewey decimal classification system divides all knowledge, as represented by books and other materials which are acquired by libraries, into nine main classes which are numbered by digits 1 to 9. Material too general to belong to any one of these classes, such as newspapers and encyclopedias, falls into a tenth class, numbered 0, which precedes the others. The classes are written as hundreds; thus, 000 is general works, 100 is philosophy, 200 is religion, 300 is social sciences, and so on. Each division is again divided into nine sections preceded by a general section; thus, 300 is social science in general, while 321 is forms of state, 322 the state and religion, 323 the relationship between states and individuals or groups, etc. Further division to bring together like materials is accomplished by the addition of digits following a decimal point. Usually, most numbers do not exceed six digits in length, i.e., three to the right of the decimal point; however, there are cases of numbers extending to nine and sometimes even more digits.

The basic classification system ranges from 000 to 999:

000-099	General works
100-199	Philosophy
200-299	Religion
300-399	Social sciences
400-499	Language
500-599	Pure sciences
600-699	Technology
700-799	Arts
800-899	Literature
900-999	History

The major divisions of the history category:

900-909	History
910-919	Geography, travels
920-929	Biography
930-939	Ancient History
940-949	Europe

950-959   Asia
960-969   Africa
970-979   North America
980-989   South America
990-999   Pacific Islands, Atlantic Islands, Arctic, and Antarctic

For the complete list of subclassifications see the *Dewey Decimal Classification and Relative Index,* 18th ed. 2 vols. (New York: Forest Press, Inc., of Lake Placid Club Education Foundation, 1970).

Library of Congress Classification

The Library of Congress classification system was adopted in 1900, three years after the Library of Congress moved from the Capitol to its new building. It changed systems in order to have a more systematic and functional arrangement of the Library's collection.

This system divides the fields of knowledge into twenty groups by assigning a letter to each and combining arabic numerals and additional letters to separate the main groups into classes and subclasses in somewhat the same way used in the Dewey decimal system. All books are divided into the following basic groups:

A   General works. Polygraphy
B   Philosophy. Psychology. Religion
C   Auxiliary Sciences of History
D   History: General and Old World
E-F   History: America
G   Geography. Anthropology. Recreation
H   Social Sciences
J   Political Science
K   Law
L   Education
M   Music and Books on Music
N   Fine Arts
P   Language and Literature
Q   Science
R   Medicine
S   Agriculture
T   Technology
U   Military Science
V   Naval Science
Z   Bibliography and Library Science

For historians, classes C through J all have some relevance. The most important categories:

CB   History of Civilization

D   History and Topography (except America)
DA   Great Britain
DB   Austria-Hungary
DC   France
DD   Germany
DE   Classical antiquity
DF   Greece
DG   Italy
DH-DJ Netherlands
DK   Russia
DL   Scandinavia
DP   Spain and Portugal
DS   Asia
DT   Africa
DU   Australia and Oceania

E 11-143   America (General)
E 150-810   United States (General, arranged chronologically)

F 1-970   United States (Local)
F 1001-1140   British North America, Canada
F 1201-1392   Mexico
F 1401-1419   Latin America (General)
F 1421-1577   Central America
F 1601-2151   West Indies
F 2201-2239   South America (General)
F 2251-3799   South America (by country)

TAKING NOTES

Now the material gathered by the student must be read and from it all pertinent information extracted. The resultant research notes should be transcribed clearly and concisely on index cards, each card marked with the title of the book or journal.

When an author is paraphrased, care should be taken to assure that his intent is not distorted; when quoting, the quote must be exact. Notes generally should be as brief as is practical, but should they run to length, the student will serve himself well to number each card used in sequence.

Finally, when the note is completed, a record should be made of the page or pages where the material was found. A word of caution: never use the back of a note card. If you avoid doing so, you will always be able to spread your information out before yourself. If you make even one exception, you may find yourself searching for a long time to locate that one note on the back of a card. It's better to make a strict rule and stick with it.

PUTTING IT ALL TOGETHER

The original material has now been read and gleaned of all material that will give some form to the preliminary skeletal outline. It is all there on the index cards, waiting to be shaped by the student. He should read the notes carefully, gaining in this manner a comprehensive overview of his material; he should become aware of supporting and contradicting material, and then—using the rough draft as a guide—he should begin mentally building the essay step by step from the information amassed.

It is at this point that the student may decide that his material indicates that a new or different tack should be taken, that more research is necessary to fill in gaps, that it is advisable to alter the original outline, perhaps drastically, or that he was on target right from the start. Whatever the decision, a final outline is cast, the one on which the facts of the research must ultimately hang. And when the dust has cleared, that new outline should contain the main theme, a list of points to be emphasized, and the placement of those points in the finished paper. It is ready to be written.

WRITING THE PAPER

The preceding steps have led to the actual writing of the first draft of the essay, and there are easily a hundred ways of attacking this task. The simplest is for the student to know what he wants to say about his topic and then to say it simply and directly. Clarity is important; when the paper is finished, there ought to be no mistaking its intent.

Setting down in order all the material gathered is not enough. The writing must reflect the writer; that is to say, it should be imbued with his thoughts on the topic, his questions of the material used, his intellectual strength in bringing opposite opinions face to face.

To wind up the demands of form, the student must remember that when quotations, opinions, or statistics are woven into the fabric of the essay, they must be acknowledged through a footnote. Also, the completed paper must contain a title page at the beginning and a bibliography at the end.

Form of the Paper

To grasp a handy maxim, neatness counts. It would be almost cavalier to spend all the time and energy that a good paper demands, and then produce a sloppy, nonuniform, slipshod copy for the instructor.

Usually an instructor requires that the paper have a suitable cover, and that its parts be arranged in a logically flowing sequence; a sequence such as the following is generally found acceptable:

1. The title page, uniformly spaced, should bear the following information.
   Title of the paper in capital letters
   Student's name
   Course and instructor
   School name
   Date
2. Dedication (optional).
3. The preface (also optional) usually acknowledges any debts the writer incurred in researching his topic.
4. The table of contents should be on a separate page and should offer the name of each chapter or division, any appendixes used, and the bibliography. Each of these sections should be identified by the page number of the paper where they are to be found. Frequently a paper is not divided into chapters and contains no index, and so it follows that a table of contents is unnecessary.
5. Illustrations, if used, should be listed on a separate page

and otherwise treated as the table of contents is treated.
6. Introduction.
7. The manuscript itself should be neatly typed on one side of white standard 8 X 11 paper. Corrected typographical errors usually are acceptable but too many make the product unworthy of the time and work invested. The body of type should be arranged neatly on each page, with plenty of room at the top and bottom and at each margin.

   The text should be double-spaced, but single-spaced verse, extended prose quotations, and footnotes are conventional. Should a quote run less than two typewritten lines, quotation marks are used.

   Finally, the page numbers, including those of the appendix and bibliography, are marked in arabic numerals in the upper right corner.
8. The bibliography often causes the undergraduate grief, so a separate section has been devoted to this subject and to footnotes.

Note: the average term paper does not include sections 2 through 6 on most occasions.

Selecting a Topic

Selecting an initial topic can be a time-consuming and frustrating task. The problem is one of developing a focus which is both interesting and workable. Hours and hours may be spent trying to formulate an approach or researching what turns out to be an unworkable topic. A topic that may be interesting ("How to Prevent World War III") is not always manageable; one that may be manageable ("Guatemalan-American Relations in 1921") might not stir the imagination. The student often must gear his topic to the holdings of his college library. Topics that are feasible at Northwestern University may not be at Minot (N. Dak.) State College.

It is important to select a topic that is interesting, not only as it is originally conceived, but one which continues to hold interest through the hard task of research. Choosing a topic and scanning the sources are not separate tasks; they are entwined—doing one helps in doing the other. In this section three important steps are presented leading to developing an interesting and workable topic.

A PRACTICAL FORMULA FOR CHOOSING A TOPIC

The first step in developing any formula is to define its elements; thus, one must first decide upon an initial area. To simplify this process possible research areas have been divided into two basic groups: the *abstract* and the *concrete*. These two general areas are further divided into subgroups.

The class textbook is usually the first place to search for a topic. For those with no idea of even a possible subject, here are some of the fertile sources in most libraries:

Encyclopedias (pp. 50-52)
Annals of European Civilization, 1501-1900 (p. 48)
The Annual Register of World Events (p. 48)
Chronology of the Modern World (p. 49)
Dictionary of American History (p. 49)
Famous First Facts (p. 53)
Historical Tables: 58 B.C.-A.D. 1965 (p. 54)
The Oxford Classical Dictionary (p. 57)
A New Dictionary of British History (p. 56)
World Almanac (p. 58)

The Concrete—Browsing For Ideas

There is a natural appeal to a concrete topic; that is to say, a topic concerned with a person or an event.

If one has a predisposition to investigate something, it is likely to be one of the above concrete items. If the idea of such a topic is appealing, but it is difficult to choose which person or country would be most interesting, an hour or so of creative browsing may be rewarding. Simply thumbing through some of the resources listed on the following pages may bring several topics to mind. The most useful and general of these sources are listed below. In most cases the title will give a general description of the work. For a more detailed description as well as the bibliographic citation, refer to the page listed after each title.

A Person
Webster's Biographical Dictionary (p. 81)
Dictionary of American Biography (p. 77)
Dictionary of National Biography (p. 78)
Who Was Who in America (p. 83)
National Cyclopedia of American Biography (p. 79)
Biographical Directory of the American Congress (p. 76)
Dictionary of Canadian Biography (p. 78)
Dictionnaire de biographie française (p. 78)
Neue deutsche Biographie (p. 80)

Who's Who in History (British) (p. 82)
Who Was When (p. 83)

An Event

An Encyclopedia of American History (p. 51)
An Encyclopedia of World History (p. 52)
The Annual Register of World Events (p. 48)
Chronology of the Modern World (p. 49)
New York Times Index (p. 73)
World Almanac (p. 58)
Guide to the Diplomatic History of the United States (p. 63)

The Abstract—Browsing for Ideas

Classifying ideas and abstractions has been the pursuit of philosophers for centuries. Since the purpose of this book is to use ideas in a practical fashion to help focus and organize the proposed paper, a very simple threefold classification will be adopted for abstract topics.

1. *Values*: ideas and concepts implying desirability
2. *Problems*: ideas and concepts implying undesirability
3. *Process*: ideas and concepts that imply neither desirability or undesirability

To be more explicit, "value" refers to any concept or idea that describes an interest, pleasure, moral obligation, desire, want, need, etc. It may refer to a measurable activity, like equal opportunity in employment, or to an intangible, such as "support for the regime."

"Problem," the second organizational classification, may also refer to a measurable activity or a feeling, but it is generally regarded as undesirable, such as a feeling of political alienation or apathy, poverty, or war.

"Process" has no connotation of desirability or undesirability but simply refers to any observable or definable pattern in activities of people and groups. "Political process" refers to the pattern that emerges from the behavior of people and groups as they strive for and use political power.

Many ideas or concepts can be placed in two or even all

three of these categories—depending upon the intent of the holder. The radical ideas of Mark Rudd, for instance, can be treated as a neutral process, a grave problem, or a boon to the Republic. How one regards these ideas depends upon his own attitudes. The categories of value, problem, and process simply help in identifying one's own feelings toward these ideas in order to use them in organizing a paper.

All three of the abstract concept classifications have one thing in common: as ideas, they cannot be seen, heard, or felt. Often they are not even recognized by those involved but are an abstraction imposed upon them by an outside observer (for example, the process of a group of grade-school children saluting the flag). Neither these children nor their teacher may realize that they are involved in the "process of political socialization" but they would be observed as such by many political scientists.

Whatever one's preference for political description, these three categories of abstract ideas will be invaluable for organizing thoughts and ideas into a paper. Since most source books deal with ideas and concepts applicable to all three categories, they have been listed together.

Abstractions: Values, Problems, and Process
The best general sources
   The *Syntopicon* volumes (p. 54)
   America: History and Life (p. 69)
   Historical Abstracts, 1775-1945 (p. 71)
   Reader's Guide to Periodical Literature (p. 73)
   Dissertations in History (p. 61)
   Social Sciences and Humanities Index (p. 74)
   International Encyclopedia of the Social Sciences (p. 55)

As one begins to explore the material it is usually discovered that far more has been written on the chosen topic than expected. The traditional advice is to "narrow" the topic, but this is only a partial answer, for "narrowing" in the traditional way can squeeze the life out of an interesting topic. The next section demonstrates how to narrow a topic and still keep it interesting.

DEVELOPING THE TOPIC

What is usually called "narrowing down" refers to the process of reducing a topic in terms of either time or space. Instead of writing about Robert Kennedy's entire life, the topic may be reduced to the months he spent working for Senator Joseph McCarthy. Instead of writing about Mexican politics, a paper on politics in Sonora Province might be developed. The project now appears to become manageable, but it may not be, actually, because one still may find that there is far more written about politics in Sonora Province or about this period in Robert Kennedy's life than can be dealt with in a term paper. When a topic is finally narrowed down, it often is so narrow that it becomes a task even to state the title. On the other hand, if it is decided not to narrow the topic down, coverage often is so superficial that originality is sacrificed.

Another choice is available in reducing a topic: that is, to develop a sharper focus in terms of interesting and worthwhile questions that might be answered about the chosen topic, questions that help to define what is relevant and what is not for research.

The problem is now to identify these questions. One method is to combine the categories of the abstract and concrete; for example, that topic of Robert Kennedy (concrete) and the idea of "Black Power" (an abstract value). There are a great many possible combinations of these categories. To help in identifying some of the possibilities for a selected topic, three charts have been constructed:

1. Combining the concrete and the abstract
2. Combining one abstraction with another
3. Combining two concrete objects

Tables 1, 2 and 3 develop these possibilities further.

TABLE 1 / Combining the Concrete and the Abstract

	Process	Problem	Value
Person	Napoleon and the introduction of efficient government	Gen. Lewis Hershey and the alienation of American youth	Will Rogers and the development of American political satire
Event	The election of 1928 and the growth of the New Deal coalition	The Treaty of Versailles and the rise of Adolph Hitler	The War of 1812 and the tradition of political dissent

TABLE 2 / Combining Two Abstractions as a Focus

	Process	Problem	Value
Process	The conflict between internal congressional and constituent pressures upon Congresswoman Shirley Chisholm	The election of federal judges and the problems of conflict of interest	The development of political attitudes in the comic strip "Peanuts"
Problem	Presidential press relations: the problem of Lyndon Johnson	Organized crime, wiretapping and the right of privacy	Rational choice in presidential elections and the threat of television image-making
Value	The impact of capital punishment on prison discipline	Adam Clayton Powell and the right of Congress to expel its members	Speed vs. thoroughness: drug testing problems of F.D.A.

TABLE 3 / Combining Two Concrete Objects of Study on the Basis of an Abstraction

	Person	Event
Person	Eugene McCarthy and Hubert Humphrey as freshman senators: a comparison	Harold Stassen and the Republican Convention of 1948
Event	Mayor Richard Daley and the election of John F. Kennedy in 1960	A comparison of two campaigns: Henry Wallace 1948, George Wallace 1968

Footnotes and Bibliography

FOOTNOTES

Few aspects of writing cause as much confusion, bewilderment, and frustration as the proper use of footnotes. Footnotes are an essential part of scholarly writing, but until the fundamentals of their use are mastered, the footnote requirement can be a constant source of frustration. As a writing device footnotes are useful because they allow important information to be communicated without overburdening the text. More specifically, footnotes allow a writer to reflect both credit and blame where they are due by showing the source of facts and ideas, thereby permitting the reader to utilize cited sources. In addition, footnotes act as a helpful context for presenting information, indicating sources from which it came, and thus allowing the reader to judge the possible bias of such sources. Finally, footnotes allow a writer to discuss interesting sidelights of the material without breaking the flow of writing.

Two questions invariably arise whenever footnotes are required:

1. What should be footnoted?
2. What form is correct, particularly if unusual or specialized material is being used, such as mimeographed campaign literature?

WHAT TO FOOTNOTE

While most style manuals or term-paper handbooks deal with footnote form, few ever touch upon the more difficult and confusing question, such as "What kind of source should I footnote and how often should I do it?" There are no ready answers to this question and unfortunately it is quite easy to succumb to excess in either direction. If one feels uneasy about an assignment, the material, or the professor's standards and expectations, it is quite tempting to "over-document" a paper or to hang footnotes on it as though one were decorating a Christmas tree. This approach can be quite hazardous, for besides wasting time, the reader is overburdened with needless side trips to the bottom of the page and the likelihood of making technical errors is increased. Such errors would, of course, detract from the substance of a paper. Unnecessary footnotes, far from being a safeguard, can become a real problem.

Equally hazardous is the practice of "under-documentation." If footnoting has always been a mystery, something to be avoided, the possibility arises that the material will be distorted: important points may be omitted in order to avoid documentation, or the source of information and ideas may be left to the reader's imagination, implying that the work of others is somehow your own. Between these two unfortunate extremes three styles of scholarship are defined: the original scholar, the scholarly summarizer, and the essayist and journalist. The style which most closely approximates the assigned type of paper should be followed. The *original scholar* form is appropriate for Ph.D. dissertations, Masters theses, honors papers, or term papers which fulfill the major portion of the requirements of a course. This style should also be used for papers consisting mainly of scholarly research from primary sources.

The *scholarly summarizer* style is appropriate for more-frequently assigned term papers which fulfill a minor portion of the requirements for a course. This type of paper usually consists of a summary, interpretation, synthesis of secondary sources.

The *essayist and journalist* style is also appropriate for many types of term papers, but in such cases the emphasis is upon the writer's own experience or interpretation. Strictly speaking, there are few ideas which are completely new; however, if the emphasis is to be on an original and creative reaction to these ideas, and not the ideas themselves or their origin, the essayist style is appropriate. This style may also be used if the paper is primarily a personal account or a narrative of events witnessed or situations in which the writer participated.

Table 4 summarizes the use of footnotes for each of the styles of scholarship.

Quotations

There is little question concerning the footnoting of direct quotations. The *original scholar* and the *scholarly summarizer* almost always footnote direct quotations. The exception for even the most scholarly styles are quotations from such items of public domain as the Bible and the Constitution. In such cases it is permissable to incorporate a general reference into the text of the material.

EXAMPLE:

There seemed little question that the proposal violated the "equal protection clause," the Fourteenth Amendment to the Constitution.

The dogmatic insistance of the neighborhood leader's position reminded one of Henry Clay's, "Sir, I would rather be right than President."

Form for quotations is covered in the next section.

The *essayist and journalist* make even greater use of the device of incorporating general references into the body of the text.

EXAMPLE:

The writer as a witness or observer: " 'Sir', Reynaud replied, 'we know that you will carry on. We would also if we saw any hope of victory.' " Winston S. Churchill, *Their Finest Hour, The Second World War* (Boston: Houghton Mifflin Co., 1949).

TABLE 4 / Three Types of Scholarship and Appropriate Footnote Use

Type of Information	Original Scholar	Scholarly Summarizer	Essayist and Journalist
Quotations	All except those quotations of common knowledge, in which case they would still be footnoted if they varied from one edition to another.	Same as original scholar.	Only if the quotation is controversial or highly significant to the text in which case the reference would be incorporated into the body of the material.
Facts 1. Controversial 2. Significant to the paper 3. Obscure	All but those which are part of common knowledge.	All controversial facts, a representative amount of significant facts to indicate the nature of sources, and only obscure facts which are central to the meaning of the paper.	Only controversial facts central to the meaning of the paper.
Commentary and Interpretation 1. Methodology	Brief bibliographical essay showing the scope of material.	Refers to other works which would contain bibliographical essays.	Only if different but similar methodology would yield significantly different results.
2. Context of opinions and sources	Brief bibliographical essay showing scope of material.	Refers to other works which would contain bibliographical essays.	Only to indicate that the author is aware of major different approaches; can be incorporated into the text.
Tangential information	Use infrequently for points which might need amplification. Generally, if it is worth writing, it should be included in the body of the text.	Only for points the absence of which might distort the meaning of the work. Again, it is preferable to place the information in the body of the text.	Rarely used except for humor.

Facts

The *original scholar* footnotes all but the most obvious facts. If in doubt he asks himself if the average mature reader would automatically be aware of the origin and authenticity of a particular fact. If not, it should be footnoted. In general, the three criteria for footnoting facts are:

1. *Controversiality*: Could honest men disagree over the authenticity or significance of this fact?
2. *Significance* to the paper: Does a significant part of your argument rest upon this fact?
3. *Obscurity*: Are the means or sources for establishing the authenticity of this fact beyond the average reader's experience or recall?

If a fact could be questioned in a scholarly paper on the basis of any of these three criteria it should be footnoted. The *scholarly summarizer* needs to footnote only a representative sampling of his significant facts. In this way, the type of sources used is indicated. Obscure facts need not be footnoted unless they are central to the significance of the paper.

The *essayist and journalist* seldom footnotes facts unless they are both controversial and significant to the basic purpose of the paper.

Commentary and Interpretation

Not every individual will read a report with the same interest. Some readers will be interested only in the main conclusions and the general thread of ideas while others will be interested in exploring in depth various aspects of the supporting evidence. Other readers will want to read the interesting sidelights found in research; some will find these sidelights a definite distraction. How is it possible for one manuscript to please such widely varying tastes?

Footnotes which comment upon and interpret data can be a partial solution to this dilemma. Such footnotes can be used for supplementary information which will be of interest to some readers. Again, the use of such footnotes varies with the style of scholarship. The *original scholar* does not want to overburden his text with a full explanation of the development of his methodology. In order fully to understand the methodology it is also important to make the scope of articles in journals or books dealing with this methodology available to the reader. Such an explanation takes the form of the bibliographical footnote.

EXAMPLE:

Cf. Glendon Schubert, "Ideologies and Attitudes, Academic and Judicial," *Journal of Politics,* XXIX (February 1967): 3-40; "Academic Ideology and the Study of Adjudication," *Saturday Review,* LXI (March 1967): 106-129; I. Howard, Jr., "On the Fluidity of Judicial Choice," *American Political Science Review,* LXII (May 1968): 43.

If library rather than empirical research is used, a similar bibliographical footnote dealing with library sources is appropriate.

EXAMPLE:

Prominent commentary on political obligations was offered by Thomas Aquinas, Locke, Rousseau, and notably T. H. Green, who may have been the first to use the term. A study of Green's thought and environment is Melvin Richter, *The Politics of Conscience: T. H. Green and His Age* (Cambridge: Harvard University Press, 1964), pp. 5-57. Also, review John Plamenatz, *Consent, Freedom, and Political Obligation,* 2nd ed. (New York: Oxford University Press, 1968).

Tangential Information

The *original scholar* also can use footnotes to provide tangential information, as in the following:

EXAMPLES:

Information concerned with research methodology: "We exclude respondents who claimed knowledge but are unable to produce a fragment of an accurate observation." Raymond E. Wolfinger and Fred I. Greenstein, "The Repeal of Fair Housing in California," *American Political Science Review,* LXII (September 1968): 955.

Meaning of words: "The Russian word for election, *vybory*, literally means choices, alternatives." Jerome M. Gilisin, "Soviet Elections as a Measure of Dissent: The Missing One Percent," *American Political Science Review,* LXII (September 1968): 815.

Clarifying Information: "It should be kept in mind that each Soviet voter casts several ballots—as many as seven—so that two million negative votes represent perhaps on the order of 500,000 to 700,000 dissenters." Jerome M. Gilisin, "Soviet Elections as a Measure of Dissent: The Missing One Percent," *American Political Science Review,* LXII (September 1968): 816.

Methodology
Context of Opinions and Sources

Where the *original scholar* uses footnotes to present a short bibliographical essay on his sources, the *scholarly summarizer* uses footnotes to point to the location of such documentation in other sources. This identification of other sources is equally useful for both library and empirical research.

EXAMPLES:

Methodological: For a useful survey of different methods that have been used to analyze roll-call data, see Lee F. Anderson, Meredith W. Watts, Jr., and Allen R. Wilcox, *Legislative Roll-Call Analysis* (Evanston, Ill.: Northwestern University Press, 1966). See also Duncan MacRae, Jr., *Issues and Parties in Legislative Voting: Methods of Statistical Analysis* (New York: Harper & Row, 1970) for a careful and systematic review of the statistical literature relevant to roll-call analysis.

From Stephen J. Brams and Michael K. O'Leary, "An Axiomatic Model of Voting Bodies," *American Political Science Review,* LXIV (June 1970): 449.

Library sources: P. W. Bridgmen is generally regarded as the father of the operational philosophy, and his intellectual indebtedness to Bentley is reflected in Bridgman, "Error, Quantum Theory, and the Observer," in Richard W. Taylor (ed.), *Life, Language, Law: Essays in Honor of Arthur F. Bentley* (Yellow Springs, Ohio: Antioch Press, 1957), pp. 125-131.

From Steven R. Brown and John Ellithorp, "Emotional Experiences in Political Groups: The Case of the McCarthy Phenomena," *American Political Science Review,* LXIV (June 1970): 349.

Context of Opinions: For this position, see Richard Wasserstrom, "Disobeying the Law," *The Journal of Philosophy,* LVIII (1961): 641-653. Also, I. Howard, Jr. "On the Fluidity of Judicial Choice," *American Political Science Review,* LXII (1968): 80.

The *scholarly summarizer* thus uses interpretative footnotes to demonstrate that he is aware of the broader scope of material, but does not feel compelled to list all of them himself.

The *essayist and journalist* is much more likely to incorporate such comments and interpretations into his text. However, if the *essayist and journalist* uses a research method, different versions of which yield highly different results, he is also compelled to make some justification of his methodology. Such justifications tend to break the flow of writing and again they can be placed in footnotes.

EXAMPLE:

"I rely for this version of the Vice-Presidential selection on the excellent and exclusive reporting of Carleton Kent, in the *Chicago Sun-Times,* reporting acknowledged by those who were present to be authentic." Theodore H. White,

The Making of the President (New York: Atheneum Publishers, 1961), p. 201.

The same instructions apply to the use of library sources.

EXAMPLE:

"One of the landmark studies in the field of business administration is *Strategy and Structure* by A. D. Chandler, Jr." Lawrence E. Fouraker and John M. Stopford, "Organization, Structure and the Multination Strategy," *Administrative Science Quarterly,* XIII (1968): 485.

Some essayists also place tangential material in footnotes as a humorous literary device.

EXAMPLE:

" 'Where did you sleep last night and the night before that?' (This last is an essay question, for the air traveler is usually able to declare, in good faith, that he has not slept at all for the past week)." C. Northcote Parkinson, *Parkinson's Law and Other Studies in Administration* (Boston: Houghton Mifflin Co., 1957), p. 108.

FOOTNOTE AND BIBLIOGRAPHY FORM

Footnote and bibliography forms are one of the few things in life in which one can justifiably be arbitrary. There is no inherent reason to use one form rather than another, except for the sake of clear communication and consistency. The works used should be cited in the same form as that used in indexes, bibliographies, or library card catalogs. In this way, a reader will be able to locate cited sources.

Following are examples of the most frequent types of footnotes and bibliographies used in a history paper, along with general comments and explanations. Most of the forms are based upon *The University of Chicago Manual of Style,* 12th ed., rev. (Chicago, Ill.: The University of Chicago Press, 1969). The Chicago manual does not specifically cover several forms such as interviews and political pamphlets. In such cases, examples given are consistent with Kate L. Turabian, *Student Guide for Writing College Papers,* 2nd ed. rev. (Chicago: The University of Chicago Press, 1969). The legal citations are based upon *A Uniform System of Citation,* 11th ed., *Harvard Law Review,* 1968.

All three styles of scholarship utilize bibliographies, but there is a slight variation between the two more scholarly styles and the *essayist and journalist.* Both the *original scholar* and the *scholarly summarizer* place their bibliographic entries in categories of written form. The most common are: books, periodicals, newspapers (sometimes combined with periodicals), government documents, dissertations, unpublished manuscripts, interviews, and letters. The *essayist and journalist* usually does not have enough citations to justify separate categories, and simply lists all of his sources alphabetically, by the last name of the author. A bibliography should include all works cited in footnotes plus any other works which were used. Works which were examined but not used should not be cited.

Footnotes, General Rules

Books Should Include:

1. Author's full name
2. Complete title
3. Editor, compiler, or translator (if any)
4. Name of series, volume or series number (if any)
5. Number of volumes
6. City, publisher, and date
7. Volume number and page number

Articles Should Include:

1. Author
2. Title of article
3. Periodical
4. Volume of periodical
5. Date and page numbers of article

Unpublished Material Should Include:

1. Author
2. Title (if any)
3. Type of material
4. Where it may be found
5. Date
6. Page number (if any)

Bibliography, General Rules

Footnote style can be changed to bibliographic style by transposing author's first and last names, removing parenthesis from facts of publication, omitting page references, and repunctuating with periods instead of commas.

Books Should Include:

1. Name of author(s), editors, or institutions responsible
2. Full title, including subtitle if one exists
3. Series, if any
4. Volume number
5. Editions, if not the original
6. Publisher's name (sometimes omitted)
7. Date of publication

Articles Should Include:

1. Name of author
2. Title of article
3. Name of periodical
4. Volume number (or date, or both)
5. Pages

Examples Contrasting Footnote and Bibliographic Forms

1. Book With One Author

FOOTNOTE: 1. George Sabine, *A History of Political Theory* (New York: Holt, Rinehart, & Winston, Inc., 1961), pp. 467-68.

BIBLIOGRAPHY: Sabine, George. *A History of Political*

Theory. New York: Holt, Rinehart, & Winston, Inc., 1961.

COMMENTS: Titles of other works appearing in the title are in quotation marks.

2. Book With Two Authors

FOOTNOTE: 2. Robert Dahl and Charles Lindblom, *Politics, Economics, and Welfare* (New York: Harper & Row, Publishers, 1953), p. 115.

BIBLIOGRAPHY: Dahl, Robert, and Lindblom, Charles. *Politics, Economics, and Welfare.* New York: Harper & Row, Publishers, 1953.

3. Book With Three Authors

FOOTNOTE: 3. John R. Meyer, John F. Kain, and Martin Wohl, *The Urban Transportation Problem* (Cambridge, Mass.: Harvard University Press, 1968), p. 50.

BIBLIOGRAPHY: Meyer, John; Kain, John F.; and Wohl, Martin. *The Urban Transportation Problem.* Cambridge, Mass.: Harvard University Press, 1968.

4. Book With More Than Three Authors

FOOTNOTE: 4. John Wahlke et al., *The Legislative System* (New York: John Wiley & Sons, Inc., 1962), p. 23.

BIBLIOGRAPHY: Wahlke, John; Eulau, Heinz; Buchanan, William; and Ferguson, LeRoy C. *The Legislative System.* New York: John Wiley & Sons, Inc., 1962.

5. Book With An Association As Author

FOOTNOTE: 5. National Manpower Council, *Government and Manpower* (New York: Columbia University Press, 1964), p. 76.

BIBLIOGRAPHY: National Manpower Council. *Government and Manpower.* New York: Columbia University Press, 1964.

6. Pseudonym, Author's Real Name Known

FOOTNOTE: 6. Samuel Clemens [Mark Twain], *Huckleberry Finn* (New York: Harcourt, Brace & World, 1969), p. 8.

BIBLIOGRAPHY: Clemens, Samuel [Mark Twain]. *Huckleberry Finn.* New York: Harcourt, Brace & World, 1969.

7. Author's Name Not on Title Page, But Known

FOOTNOTE: 7. [Alexander Hamilton, James Madison, and John Jay], *The Federalist Papers,* ed. Jacob Cook (Middletown, Conn.: Wesleyan University Press, 1961), p. 182.

BIBLIOGRAPHY: [Hamilton, Alexander; Madison, James; and Jay, John.] *The Federalist Papers.* Edited by Jacob Cook. Middletown, Conn.: Wesleyan University Press, 1961.

8. Book's Author Anonymous

FOOTNOTE: 8. *The Holy Quran* (Washington, D.C.: Islamic Center, 1960), p. 177.

BIBLIOGRAPHY: *The Holy Quran.* Washington, D.C.: Islamic Center, 1960.

COMMENTS: Avoid use of "Anon." or "Anonymous."

9. Book By Editor, Compiler or Translator: No Other Author Listed

Editors

FOOTNOTE: 9. Robert Theobold, ed., *Social Policies for America in the Seventies: Nine Divergent Views* (New York: Doubleday & Co., Inc., 1968), p. 85.

BIBLIOGRAPHY: Theobold, Robert, ed. *Social Policies for America in the Seventies: Nine Divergent Views.* New York: Doubleday & Co., Inc., 1968.

Compilers

FOOTNOTE: 10. Robert Lindsay and John Neu, comps., *French Political Pamphlets, 1547-1684* (Madison: University of Wisconsin Press, 1969), p. 8.

BIBLIOGRAPHY: Lindsay, Robert, and Neu, John, comps. *French Political Pamphlets, 1547-1684.* Madison: University of Wisconsin Press, 1969.

Translators

FOOTNOTE: 11. Ursule Molinaro, trans., *Beowulf* (New York: Farrar, Straus, & Giroux, Inc., 1957), p. 23.

BIBLIOGRAPHY: Molinaro, Ursule, trans. *Beowulf.* New York: Farrar, Straus, & Giroux, Inc., 1957.

10. Translated or Edited Books in Which the Author is Known

FOOTNOTE: 12. Gustav Stolper, Karl Hausel, and Knut Borchardt, *The German Economy, 1870 to Present,* trans. Toni Stoper (New York: Harcourt, Brace & World, 1969), pp. 8-10.

BIBLIOGRAPHY: Stolper, Gustav; Hausel, Karl; and Borchardt, Knut. *The German Economy, 1870 to Present.* Translated by Toni Stoper. New York: Harcourt, Brace, & World, 1969.

11. Edited or Translated Work in Which the Editor is More Important than the Author

FOOTNOTE: 13. William L. Riordon, ed., *Plunkitt of Tammany Hall,* by George Washington Plunkitt (New York: E. P. Dutton & Co., 1900), p. 25.

BIBLIOGRAPHY: Riordon, William L., ed. *Plunkitt of Tammany Hall,* by George Washington Plunkitt. New York: E. P. Dutton & Co., 1900.

12. Books, Multivolume

FOOTNOTE: 14. Fred E. Inbau, James R. Thompson, and Claude R. Sowle, *Cases and Comments on Criminal Justice,* 3 vols. (Mineola, N.Y.: The Foundation Press, Inc., 1968), 1:5.

BIBLIOGRAPHY: Inbau, Fred E.; Thompson, James R.; and Sowle, Claude R. *Cases and Comments on Criminal Justice.* Vol. 1. Mineola, N.Y.: The Foundation Press, Inc., 1968.

13. Book in a Series

FOOTNOTE: 15. W. F. Gutteridge, *The Military in African Politics,* Studies in African History (London: Methuen & Co. Ltd., 1969), p. 22.

BIBLIOGRAPHY: Gutteridge, W. F. *The Military in African Politics.* Studies in African History. London: Methuen & Co. Ltd., 1969.

COMMENTS: If a book is part of a series the citations

should include the name of the series and the volume number. Spell out the author's name in full unless he is commonly known by his initials, e.g., W. F. Gutteridge.

14. Book in a Series, One Author, Several Volumes, Each With a Different Title

FOOTNOTE: 16. Charles Edward Mallet, *The Medieval University and Colleges Founded in the Middle Ages,* 3 vols., The History of Oxford University (New York: Barnes & Noble, Inc., 1968), 1:23.

BIBLIOGRAPHY: Mallet, Charles Edward. *The Medieval University and Colleges Founded in the Middle Ages.* Vol. 1. The History of Oxford University. New York: Barnes & Noble, Inc., 1968.

15. Paperback Edition of a Book First Published in Hard Cover

FOOTNOTE: 17. Aaron Wildavsky, *The Politics of the Budgetary Process* (Boston: Little, Brown and Co., paperback, 1964), p. 177.

BIBLIOGRAPHY: Wildavsky, Aaron. *The Politics of the Budgetary Process.* Boston: Little, Brown and Co., paperback, 1964.

16. Introduction to Book by Another Author

FOOTNOTE: 18. Alex Inkeles, Introduction to *The Process of Modernization,* by John Brode (Cambridge: Harvard University Press, 1969), p. vii.

BIBLIOGRAPHY: Inkeles, Alex. Introduction to *The Process of Modernization,* by John Brode. Cambridge: Harvard University Press, 1969.

17. Citation in One Book from Another Book

FOOTNOTE: 19. Jakob Hegemann, *Entlarvte Geschichte,* p. 210, as quoted in John W. Wheeler-Bennett, *The Nemesis of Power* (London: Macmillan & Co., Ltd., 1954), p. 8.

BIBLIOGRAPHY: Wheeler-Bennett, John W. *The Nemesis of Power.* London: Macmillan & Co., Ltd., 1954.

18. Book Review

FOOTNOTE: 20. Willard Ranger, "International Politics, Law, and Organization," review of *Regionalism and World Order*, by Ronald Yalem, *The American Political Science Review* 60 (September 1966): 759.

BIBLIOGRAPHY: Ranger, Willard. "International Politics, Law, and Organization," review of *Regionalism and World Order*, by Ronald Yalem. *The American Political Science Review* 60 (September 1966): 759.

19. Literature

Plays and Long Poems

FOOTNOTE: 21. George Bernard Shaw, *The Devil's Disciple* (Baltimore: Penguin Books, 1956), act 2, sc. 1, lines 8-11.

BIBLIOGRAPHY: Shaw, George Bernard. *The Devil's Disciple*. Baltimore: Penguin Books, 1956.

Short Poems

FOOTNOTE: 22. Edgar Allan Poe, "To Helen," *Eternal Passion in English Poetry* (Freeport, N.Y.: Books for Libraries, Inc., 1969), lines 3-5.

BIBLIOGRAPHY: Poe, Edgar Allan. "To Helen." *Eternal Passion in English Poetry*. Freeport, N.Y.: Books for Libraries, Inc., 1969.

20. Bible

FOOTNOTE: 23. Ruth 12:18.

BIBLIOGRAPHY: The Bible. Revised Standard Version.

21. Classical Works

FOOTNOTE: 24. Julius Caesar *The Conquest of Gaul* 1,3-5.

BIBLIOGRAPHY: Caesar, Julius. *The Conquest of Gaul* 1.

22. Modern Edition of Classical Work

FOOTNOTE: 25. Augustine *City of God* (trans. Healey-Tasker) 20.3.

BIBLIOGRAPHY: Augustine. *City of God.* Translated by Healey-Tasker. New York: Modern Library, 1952.

23. Article, Chapter, or Other Part of a Book

FOOTNOTE: 26. Leonard D. White, "The Role of the City Manager," *Urban Government,* rev. ed., edited by Edward C. Banfield (New York: The Free Press, 1969), p. 286.

BIBLIOGRAPHY: White, Leonard D. "The Role of the City Manager." *Urban Government,* rev. ed. Edited by Edward C. Banfield. New York: The Free Press, 1969.

24. Works Available in Microfilm

FOOTNOTE: 27. Abraham Tauber, *Spelling Reform in the United States* (Ann Arbor, Mich.: University Microfilms, 1958).

BIBLIOGRAPHY: Tauber, Abraham. *Spelling Reform in the United States.* Ann Arbor, Mich.: University Microfilms, 1958.

25. Encyclopedias, Almanacs, and Other Reference Works
Signed Articles

FOOTNOTE: 28. *International Encyclopedia of the Social Sciences,* 5th ed., s.v. "Systems Analysis: Political Systems," by William C. Mitchell.

BIBLIOGRAPHY: *International Encyclopedia of the Social Sciences,* 5th ed., s.v. "Systems Analysis: Political Systems," by William C. Mitchell.

Unsigned Articles

FOOTNOTE: 29. *Oxford Dictionary of National Biography,* 2nd ed., s.v. "Akers-Douglas, Aretas."

BIBLIOGRAPHY: *Oxford Dictionary of National Biography,* 2nd ed., s.v. "Akers-Douglas, Aretas."

26. Periodical: Author Given
Consecutive Pages

FOOTNOTE: 30. David Fellman, "Constitutional Law in 1958-1959," *American Political Science Review* 54 (1960): 168-70.

BIBLIOGRAPHY: Fellman, David. "Constitutional Law in 1958-1959." *American Political Science Review* 54 (1960): 168-70.

Nonconsecutive Pages

FOOTNOTE: 31. Will Lissner, "Protection of the Author's Reprint Rights," *American Journal of Economics* 28 (April 1969): 2,11.

BIBLIOGRAPHY: Lissner, Will. "Protection of the Author's Reprint Rights." *American Journal of Economics* 28 (April 1968): 2,11.

27. Magazine Article, No Author Given

FOOTNOTE: 32. "Tax Changes for 1971: The Plans Take Shape," *U.S. News & World Report,* 5 October 1970, p. 91.

BIBLIOGRAPHY: "Tax Changes for 1971: The Plans Take Shape." *U.S. News & World Report,* 5 October 1970, p. 91.

28. Newspapers

American

FOOTNOTE: 33. George C. Wilson, "Copter Force Hits Camp Near Hanoi," *The Washington Post,* 24 November 1970, p. 1A.

BIBLIOGRAPHY: Wilson, George C, "Copter Force Hits Camp Near Hanoi," *The Washington Post* 351 (24 November 1970): 1A.

Foreign

FOOTNOTE: 34. *Times* (London), 1 December 1970, p. 10.

BIBLIOGRAPHY: *Times* (London), 1 December 1970, p. 10.

COMMENTS: Include name of city for foreign newspapers.

29. Proceedings of a Meeting or Conference: Reproduced

FOOTNOTE: 35. The Seventy-seventh Annual Conference of the International Chiefs of Police, "Proceedings of the Conference of the International Chiefs of Police," mimeographed (Atlantic City: C.I.C.P., October 6, 1970), p. 2.

BIBLIOGRAPHY: The Seventy-seventh Annual Conference of the International Chiefs of Police. "Proceedings of the Conference of the International Chiefs of Police." Atlantic City: C.I.C.P. October 6, 1970. Mimeographed.

30. Minutes of a Meeting: Not Reproduced

FOOTNOTE: 36. Minutes of Meeting Capitol Improvement Advisory Committee, Washington, D.C., 5 May 1971, p. 2.

BIBLIOGRAPHY: Capitol Improvement Advisory Committee. Washington, D.C. Minutes of Meeting of 5 May 1971

31. Paper Read or Speech Delivered at a Meeting

FOOTNOTE: 37. John N. Mitchell, "Legalized Wiretapping" (Address delivered at the Seventy-seventh Annual Conference of the International Chiefs of Police, Atlantic City, October 5, 1970), p. 5.

BIBLIOGRAPHY: Mitchell, John N. "Legalized Wiretapping." Address delivered at the Seventy-seventh Annual Conference of International Chiefs of Police, October 5, 1970, at Atlantic City, N.J. Mimeographed.

32. Thesis or Dissertation

FOOTNOTE: 38. William John Thomson, "Variables Affecting Human Discrimination Processes" (Ph.D. diss., Stanford University, 1969), p. 87.

BIBLIOGRAPHY: Thomson, William John. "Variables Affecting Human Discrimination Processes." Ph.D. dissertation, Stanford University, 1969.

33. Legal Citations
Federal Statute

FOOTNOTE: 39. *Administrative Procedure Act,* @ 11-6 U.S.C. @ 1009 (1964).

BIBLIOGRAPHY: *Administrative Procedure Act.*@11-6 U.S.C.@1009 (1964).

State Statute
FOOTNOTE: 40. *Blue Sky Law,@2* New York General Business Code @ 352, (McKinney, 1962).
BIBLIOGRAPHY: *Blue Sky Law.@2* New York General Business Code@352, McKinney, 1962.

Court Case
FOOTNOTE: 41. *Kerr v. California,* 357 U.S. 50 (1963).
BIBLIOGRAPHY: *Kerr v. California,* 357 U.S. 50 (1963).

Law Review Articles
FOOTNOTE: 42. L. C. Ebb, *The Grundig-Consten Case Revisited,* 115 Univ. Penn. L. Rev., 885 (1969).
BIBLIOGRAPHY: Ebb, L. C. *The Grundig-Consten Case Revisited.* 115 Univ. Penn. L. Rev., 1969.

Statutory Material
FOOTNOTE: 43. U.S., *Constitution,* art. 2, sec. 1.
BIBLIOGRAPHY: U.S. *Constitution,* art. 2, sec. 1.

34. Material from Manuscript Collections
FOOTNOTE: 44. Diary of Lewis Tappan, 23 February 1836 to 29 August 1838, Tappan Papers, Library of Congress, Washington, D.C.
BIBLIOGRAPHY: Washington, D.C. Library of Congress. Tappan Papers. Diary of Lewis Tappan, 23 February 1836 to 29 August 1838.

35. Radio and Television Programs
FOOTNOTE: 45. C.B.S., "C.B.S. Evening News," 8 December 1970, "Rube Goldberg Dies," Walter Cronkite, reporter.
BIBLIOGRAPHY: C.B.S. "C.B.S. Evening News," 8 December 1970, "Rube Goldberg Dies," Walter Cronkite, reporter.

36. Interview
FOOTNOTE: 46. Interview with Mr. Carl Rauh, Deputy Attorney General for the District of Columbia, Washington, December 2, 1970.

BIBLIOGRAPHY: Rauh, Carl, Deputy Attorney General for the District of Columbia. Washington. Interview, December 2, 1970.

37. Mimeographed or Other Nonprinted Reports
FOOTNOTE: 47. American University, "Codebook: Baker Survey of Local Elected Officials," mimeographed (Washington: American University School of Government), p. 5.

BIBLIOGRAPHY: American University. "Codebook: Baker Survey of Local Elected Officials." Mimeographed. Washington: American University School of Government.

38. Pamphlet
FOOTNOTE: 48. Harold T. Effer, *Joseph Clark, Your Man in Washington,* Office of Sen. Clark (Washington, D.C., Fall, 1968), p. 2.

BIBLIOGRAPHY: Effer, Harold T. *Joseph Clark, Your Man in Washington.* Office of Sen. Clark. Washington, D.C., Fall, 1968.

39. Letters
FOOTNOTE: 49. Lawrence to Barr, 8 November 1958, Political Papers of Governor David Leo Lawrence, Hillman Library, University of Pittsburgh, Pittsburgh, Pa.

BIBLIOGRAPHY: Pittsburgh, Pa. Hillman Library. University of Pittsburgh. Political Papers of Governor David Leo Lawrence. Lawrence to Barr, 8 November 1958.

40. Documents
Citing documents is always a difficult problem, for their form is totally unlike that of books and magazines. The card catalog is a good guide and the following general rules should help. Include in this order:

1. The country (U.S. etc.)
2. Branch of Government (Legislative, executive, etc.)
3. The subbranch or subbranches (House, Committee on Education and Labor, etc.)

The branches of subbranches can become complicated: a careful examination of the document itself, its entry is the card catalog or the *Government Organization Manual* should give you an idea as to the sequence of organization.

This information is followed by the title (underlined), the name of the series or sequence, and the facts of publication. The following examples include the most commonly cited government publications.

41. Congressional Documents
Bills

FOOTNOTE: 50. U.S., Congress, House, *Higher Education Act of 1965,* 89th Cong., 1st sess.,1965, H.R. 9567, p. 37.

BIBLIOGRAPHY: U.S. Congress. House. *Higher Education Act of 1965.* 89th Cong., 1st sess., H.R. 9567.

FOOTNOTE: 51. U.S., Congress, Senate, *Metropolitan Planning Act,* 88th Cong., 2nd sess., 1964, S. 855.

BIBLIOGRAPHY: U.S. Congress. Senate. *Metropolitan Planning Act.* 88th Cong., 2nd sess., S. 885.

Debates

FOOTNOTES: 52. U.S., Congress, Senate, *Congressional Record,* 91st Cong., 2nd sess., 1970, 25, pt. 511:665.

BIBLIOGRAPHY: U.S. Congress. Senate. *Congressional Record,* 91st Cong, 2nd sess., 1970, 25, pt. 511:665.

Report

FOOTNOTE: 53. U.S., Congress, House, *Higher Education Act of 1965,* 89th Cong., 1st sess., 1965, H. Rept. 621 to accompany H.R. 9567.

BIBLIOGRAPHY: U.S. Congress. House. *Higher Education Act of 1965,* 89th Cong., 1st sess., 1965, H.R. 9567.

Hearings

FOOTNOTE: 54. U.S., Congress, House, Committee on Ways and Means, *Hearings to Exclude from the Gross Income the First $750 of Interest Received on Deposit in Thrift Institutions, H.R. 16545,* 91st Cong.,2nd sess.,1970.

BIBLIOGRAPHY: U.S. Congress. House. Committee on Ways and Means. *Hearings to Exclude from the Gross Income the First $750 of Interest Received on Deposit in Thrift Institutions, H.R. 16545,* 91st Cong., 2nd sess., 1970.

42. Executive Documents
From an Executive Department
FOOTNOTE: 55. U.S., Department of Interior, *Final Report to the President on the Potomac Basin: "The Nation's River"* (Washington, D.C.: U.S. Dept. of Interior, 1968), p. 6.

BIBLIOGRAPHY: U.S. Department of Interior. *Final Report to the President on the Potomac Basin: "The Nation's River."* Washington, D.C.: U.S. Dept. of Interior, 1968.

Presidential Papers
FOOTNOTE: 56. U.S., President, "Statement by the President on Actions and Recommendations for the Federal City, January 31, 1969," *Weekly Compilation of Presidential Documents,* vol. 5, no. 5, February 3, 1970, p. 198.

BIBLIOGRAPHY: U.S. President. "Statement by the President on Actions and Recommendations for the Federal City, January 31, 1969." *Weekly Compilation of Presidential Documents,* 5. February 3, 1970.

43. International Documents
International Organizations
FOOTNOTE: 57. League of Nations, Secretariat, *Administration of Territory* (O.J.), March, 1920, p. 52.

BIBLIOGRAPHY: League of Nations. Secretariat. *Administration of Territory* (O.J.). March, 1920.

FOOTNOTE: 58. United Nations, Economic and Social Council, 54th Session, *Convention and Protocol for the Protection of Cultural Property in Event of Armed Conflict* (E/CL 1374), 7 July 1959, p. 2.

BIBLIOGRAPHY: United Nations. Economic and Social Council, 54th Session. *Convention and Protocol for the Protection of Cultural Property in Event of Armed Conflict* (E/CL 1374), 7 July 1959.

FOOTNOTE: 59. United Nations, General Assembly, November 20, 1959, *General Assembly Resolution 1386,* A/4353, Annex 16, pp. 19-21.

BIBLIOGRAPHY: United Nations. General Assembly. 14th Session, November 20, 1959. *General Assembly Resolution 1386,* A/4353.

Treaties

FOOTNOTE: 60. U.S., *Statutes at Large,* vol. 43, pt. 2 (December 1923 — March 1925), "Naval Arms Limitation Treaty," February 26, 1922, ch. 1, art. 1, p. 1655.

BIBLIOGRAPHY: U.S. *Statutes at Large,* vol. 43, pt. 2 (December 1923 — March 1925). "Naval Arms Limitation Treaty," February 26, 1922.

44. State and Local Documents

State

FOOTNOTE: 61. New Jersey, Office of the Governor, Governor's Select Commission on Civil Disorder, *Report for Action* (Trenton: Office of the Governor, 1968), p. 14.

BIBLIOGRAPHY: New Jersey. Office of the Governor. Governor's Select Commission on Civil Disorder. *Report for Action.* Trenton: Office of the Governor, 1968.

City

FOOTNOTE: 62. New York, N.Y., Mayor's Office, Mayor's Task Force on Reorganization of New York City Government. *The Mayor's Task Force on Reorganization of New York City Government: Report and Proposed Local Law* (New York: Institute of Public Administration, 1966), p. 9.

BIBLIOGRAPHY: New York, N.Y. Mayor's Office. Mayor's Task Force on Reorganization of New York City Government. *The Mayor's Task Force on Reorganization of New York City Government: Report and Proposed Local Law.* New York: Institute of Public Administration, 1966.

Second or Later References to Footnotes

Chances are several references will be made to the same footnote. The general rules are as follows:

1. For references to the same work with no intervening footnotes simply use the Latin term *"Ibid.,"* meaning in the same place. Note that *"Ibid."* is italicized.
2. For second references with no intervening footnote, but with a different page of the same work, state *ibid.* and the page number. *Ibid.* should be capitalized at the beginning of footnotes.

EXAMPLE: *Ibid.,* p. 87.

3. For second references with intervening footnotes state: the author's last name, but not first name or initials unless another author of the same last name is cited; a shortened title of the work and the specific page number.

Following are examples of second citations of a representative number of works.

Second References with Intervening Citations
Book, Single Volume
FIRST CITATION: 63. Thomas E. Skidmore, *Politics in Brazil* (New York: Oxford University Press, Inc., 1967), p. 81.

SECOND CITATION: 64. Thomas E. Skidmore, *Politics in Brazil,* p. 92.

Multivolume
FIRST CITATION: 65. Fred E. Inbau, James R. Thomas, and Claude R. Sowle, *Cases and Comments on Criminal Justice,* 3 vols., (Mineola, N.Y.: The Foundation Press, Inc. 1968) 1:5.

SECOND CITATION: 66. Inbau, Thomas, and Sowle, *Cases and Comments on Criminal Justice,* 1:8.

Article in Anthology
FIRST CITATION: 67. Ronald Cohen, "Anthropology and Political Science: Courtship and Marriage?" *Politics and the Social Sciences,* ed. Seymour M. Lipset (New York: Oxford University Press, Inc., 1969), p. 22.

SECOND CITATION: 68. Cohen, "Anthropology and Political Science," p. 23.

Journal Article
FIRST CITATION: 69. David Fellman, "Constitutional Law in 1958-1959," *American Political Science Review* 54 (1960): 168.

SECOND CITATION: 70. Fellman, "Constitutional Law," p. 171.

Book with an Editor or Translator, Author Unknown
FIRST CITATION: 71. Robert Theobold, ed., *Social Policies for America in the Seventies: Nine Divergent Views* (Garden City, N.Y.: Doubleday & Co., Inc., 1968), p. 3.

SECOND CITATION: 72. Theobold, ed., *Social Policies in Seventies,* p. 4.

Classical
FIRST CITATION: 73. Thucydides, *History of the Peloponnesian Wars,* 2.30, 2.

SECOND CITATION: 74. Thucy., 2.28, 1-6.

Letters
FIRST CITATION: 75. Stevens to Sumner, 28 August 1865, Charles Sumner Papers, Harvard College Library, Cambridge, Mass.

SECOND CITATION: 76. Stevens to Sumner, 28 August 1865, Sumner Papers.

State Documents
FIRST CITATION: 77. Maryland, *Ordinance Number 438* (1965) sec. 8.

SECOND CITATION: 78. Maryland, *Ordinance Number 438,* sec. 8.

Federal Document
FIRST CITATION: 79. U.S., *Statutes at Large,* vol. 43, pt. 2 (Dec. 1923-March 1925), "Naval Arms Limitation Treaty," Feb. 26, 1922, ch. 1, art. 1, p. 1655.

SECOND CITATION: 80. U.S., *Statutes at Large,* vol. 43, "Naval Arms Limitation Treaty," p. 1657.

Part II

ANNOTATED LISTING
OF BASIC REFERENCES

Annotated Listing of Basic References

A. ENCYCLOPEDIAS, DICTIONARIES, ALMANACS, AND OTHER REFERENCE SOURCES

Africa: A Handbook to the Continent. Colin Legum, ed. New York: Praeger, 1966.

An important reference work on Africa. Part I comprises chapters on individual countries. Part II treats art, literature, religion, cultural patterns, economics, and great power attitudes toward Africa. It is written in essay form and has valuable short histories of each country, but for detailed data *Africa South of the Sahara* is far more comprehensive and up to date.

Africa South of the Sahara. London: Europa Publications, 1971—. Annual.

Provides an introduction to the political, economic, and physical structure of the sub-Saharan states and territories of Africa. (*The Middle East and North Africa* treats the northern nations.) It includes scholarly background articles, appraisals of regional organizations, and a "Who's Who" south of the Sahara. The bulk of the volume is made up of detailed analyses of each nation, including geography, recent history, statistics, a directory of important political, economic, and social organizations, and a select bibliography.

The American Negro Reference Book. John P. Davis, ed. Englewood Cliffs, N. J.: Prentice-Hall, 1966.

Twenty-four scholars contributed to this specialized volume. Its purpose is to collect "a reliable summary of current information on the main aspects of Negro life in America and to present this information in sufficient historical depth to provide the reader with a fine perspective" (p. v). Most of the twenty-five chapters include bibliographical references to facilitate further inquiry, and the extensive index makes the book useful for specific questions. The volume includes 122 tables of precise statistical information. The articles vary in length, with John Hope Franklin's ninety-five page "A Brief History of the Negro in the United States" the longest.

Annals of European Civilization, 1501-1900. Alfred Mayer, ed. London: Cassell, 1949.

This chronology deals primarily with the cultural history of Europe. Events are arranged by country under the year. It includes indexes of names and places (citations of famous paintings include their present location) and topical chronologies for the specialist. A sampling of topics includes astronomy, church, history, literature, mathematics, music, painting, and philosophy. This source is excellent for the student seeking to escape the political/economic emphasis usually evidenced by such works.

The Annual Register of World Events: A Review of the Year. London: Various publishers, 1758–. Annual.

The Annual Register, a British publication and one of the best summaries of year-by-year events, emphasizes Great Britain and the Commonwealth. It also covers such areas as political, economic, and cultural events and speeches from around the world, with summaries, maps, sketches, graphs, and an index to names. The essays are well written by specialists.

Asia: A Handbook. Guy Wint, ed. New York: Praeger, 1966.

A one-volume reference work for the region east of Iran prepared by over sixty authorities. It treats most aspects of the area. One section has a statistical analysis of each country; a second, the history and present status of each country; the third treats broader cultural patterns. Appendices include postwar treaties and a bibliography of American publications on the region. The volume is less statistical and more literary than Europa's *The Far East and Australasia.*

Chronology of the Modern World: 1763 to the Present Time. Neville Williams. New York: David McKay Co., 1966.

Covers "the events and achievements in every walk of life of the past two centuries" (p. ix). In addition to the chronological main body of the book, an extensive index readily facilitates the location of specific references. The left-hand page deals with political and international events, the right with the arts and sciences, which are subdivided under twelve classified headings. The book enables the student to relate events to their chronological context.

Congressional Quarterly Almanac. Washington, D. C.: Congressional Quarterly, Inc., 1945–. Annual.

Based on the *CQ Weekly Report,* the *CQ Almanac* is published each spring as a complete record of the legislation of the past session of Congress. The bulk of the volume deals with Congressional action. The detailed table of contents includes many specific topics under the main headings: Agriculture and Labor, Appropriations, Education and Health, Foreign Policy, General Government, National Security, Resources and Public Works, Transportation and Communication, Taxes and Economic Policy, and Welfare and Urban Affairs. A thorough subject and name index, roll-call charts, presidential messages, action on presidential appointments, and objective analytic articles about various facets of government operations during the year add to its value. That the *CQ Almanac* is well written and pleasant to read is a delightful fringe benefit.

Dictionary of American History. James Truslow Adams, ed. 5 vols. plus index. New York: C. Scribners' Sons, 1942-61. *Supplement One,* 1961.

The most comprehensive reference work for American history. It contains over 6000 alphabetical entries dealing with all but biographical facets of the nation's past from 1600 to 1940. It was originally designed to pull together the masses of new information unearthed by historians in the early twentieth century. The articles, usually brief, are signed by contributing specialists. Cross references facilitate deeper searches and a detailed index volume leads the reader to specific aspects of a subject. The supplemental volume brings the series up to 1960.

Encyclopedia Americana. New York: The Americana Corporation, 1973.

One of the two best general encyclopedias, *Americana* is strongest as a quick reference source for all aspects of American life and culture, particularly recent American history. The index volume contains a useful illustrated chronology of world events for the five years preceding publication. Articles conclude with extensive and authoritative bibliographies. An annual supplement keeps the set up to date.

Encyclopaedia Britannica. Chicago: Encyclopaedia Britannica Inc., 1973.

No longer British oriented, this is without question the single most extensive and detailed general encyclopedia, with some articles in the traditional fields of the humanities, arts, and sciences that have become classics. In scope and depth the major articles are equivalent to specialized books on the subject, but unlike ordinary books a *Britannica* article is assuredly written by an outstanding authority in his field. The assistance of cross references and "sign post" articles to lead to related material in other fields is also given.

The Encyclopedia of American Facts and Dates. Gorton Carruth, ed. New York: Thomas Y. Crowell, 1966.

Divides historical topics into four categories and arranges the four concurrently. Column one deals with politics, government, war, vital statistics, and related matters. Column two covers literature, art and popular thought. The third column includes economics, science, education, religion, philosophy, and business affairs. Column four treats popular entertainment, society, and sports. The writing is entertaining as well as informative, and thoroughly indexed to increase its value.

Encyclopedia of American History. Richard B. Morris, ed. New York: Harper and Row, 1965.

This one-volume work thoroughly covers American history. Part I is a detailed chronology of major political and military events. Part II is a topical chronology of expansion, demography, constitutional development, economics, science, and thought. The different approaches of the first two sections make it convenient to investigate either general affairs or specific themes. Part III contains brief biographies of 400 notable Americans and offers a starting point for more detailed research on them. The lack of a bibliography is a shortcoming, but overall this is a very useful reference tool.

The Encyclopedia of Islam. H. A. R. Gibb, et al., eds. 5 vols. Leiden: E. J. Brill, Ltd., 1960–.

The most thorough source of information on Islamic civilization. The first edition, issued in four volumes in 1913-1934, is being updated at present. Scholarly and authoritative, the signed articles (with bibliographies) cover a vast array of topics, especially the geography, ethnography, and biography of the Muhammadan peoples. This is the indispensable tool for the student interested in Islam.

Encyclopedia of Latin-American History. Michael R. Martin and Gabriel H. Lovett, eds. Rev. ed. by Robert Hughes. Indianapolis: Bobbs-Merrill Co., 1968.

A convenient one-volume treatment of the sweep of Latin American history from the pre-Columbian period to the present. It treats European colonization, the political, social, and economic development of Latin American nations, foreign relations within and without the region, cities, wars, governments, economic developments, and biographies of notable figures. It also includes definitions of significant Portuguese and Spanish words and phrases. Entries are arranged alphabetically.

The Encyclopedia of Military History from 3500 B.C. to the Present. R. Ernest Dupuy and Trevor N. Dupuy. New York: Harper and Row, 1970.

A reference work for the entire sweep of world military

history. It is organized into a series of chronologically and geographically framed narratives of wars, warfare, and military affairs. Each of the twenty-one time periods is introduced by an essay assessing the principal military trends of the period, including leaders, weapons, tactics, and strategy. An exhaustive index of names and events is supplemented by a special index for wars and one for battles and seiges. An eight-page bibliography directs the student to more specialized works.

Encyclopedia of the Social Sciences. Edwin R. A. Seligman, ed. 15 vols. New York: Macmillan, 1930-35.

Hundreds of international scholars prepared this comprehensive survey of the fields of social science in the early 1930s, and it has remained the leader in its field. It deals with history "only to the extent that historical episodes or methods are of especial importance to the student of society." The lengthy articles, prepared by specialists, include excellent bibliographies. About half the articles are biographical. Somewhat out of date today, it should be used with the newer *International Encyclopedia of the Social Sciences.*

An Encyclopedia of World History. William L. Langer, ed. Boston: Houghton-Mifflin, 1968.

In no other volume can one locate the essential facts of world history so quickly. Using an expanded outline form with important names and dates in boldface type, this single volume covers the recorded history of the world. Extensively indexed, it allows one to spend a minimum of effort in finding such data as the chronology of the short Soviet-Finno War of 1939-40 or the Moslem conquest of Spain. Outline maps and genealogical tables are scattered through the text. Appendices include lists of Roman emperors, Byzantine emperors, caliphs up to 1256, Roman popes, British and French kings, Holy Roman emperors, American presidents, United Nations members, and European and American colleges founded prior to 1900.

The Europa Yearbook: A World Survey. London: Europa Publications, 1926—. Annual.

A two-volume work offering a comprehensive treatment of

educational, economic, political, religious, and social activities throughout the world. Volume I deals with international organizations and Europe (including Russia and Turkey); Volume II covers Africa, the Americas, Asia and Australasia. Treatment is somewhat less detailed than in the regional Europa volumes, but the mass of information included is staggering. Brief introductory essays are followed by detailed statistical analyses of many aspects of every nation.

Facts about the Presidents: A Compilation of Biographical and Historical Data. Joseph Nathan Kane. New York: H. W. Wilson Co., 1968.

A fascinating collection of information about each President through Lyndon Johnson. Part I includes a standardized format for the presentation of biographical data, arranged by individual, and Part II compares the whole group of thirty-six Presidents on such facts as birthplace, father's occupation, nicknames, religious affiliation, ancestry, and a long list of others.

Famous First Facts: A Record of First Happenings, Discoveries, and Inventions in the United States. Joseph Nathan Kane. New York: H. W. Wilson Co., 1964.

Lists thousands of firsts in the United States, ranging from the momentous to the trivial. Four indexes—by year, date, personal name, and geographical location—enable the student to approach his subject from a variety of angles.

The Far East and Australasia. London: Europa Publications, 1969–. Annual.

A survey and directory of the nations from Afghanistan eastward to Siberia and New Zealand. It includes introductory articles on religion, economics, and geopolitics, analysis of regional organizations, and a "Who's Who" of the region. The main body of the book is a nation-by-nation survey divided into the regions of South Asia, South-East Asia, East Asia, and Australasia and the Pacific Islands. The national surveys parallel those in *Africa South of the Sahara.*

Foreign Relations of the United States: Diplomatic Papers.
Washington, D. C.: Government Printing Office, 1852–.

This Department of State series offers the most complete
State Department records of the past. Published after a roughly
twenty-year "cooling-off" period, the volumes list a year-by-
year selection of public documents, diplomatic correspondence,
messages between the United States and other governments, and
departmental memoranda. Each volume is thoroughly indexed.
The series is essential to the student of American diplomatic
history.

*Great Books of the Western World and the Great Ideas: A
Syntopicon.* Mortimer J. Adler, ed. Chicago: Encyclopaedia
Britannica Inc., 1961.

The two-volume *Syntopicon* contains a lengthy analytic
essay for each of the 102 "great ideas." These essays break
down and analyze each idea, illustrating in the process the
intellectual handles of each. Under "law," for instance, is a clear
and succinct approach to the idea of law—divine and natural law
and the relationship of law and the individual. The remaining
fifty-one volumes contain works of the great thinkers and
writers of Western civilization. To these fifty-one volumes the
essays of the *Syntopicon* are keyed, permitting one to trace the
development of an idea through history or to compare the views
of two or more giants of history. Each of the 102 essays is
cross-indexed, providing innumerable approaches to a single
subject.

Historical Tables: 58 B.C.-A.D. 1965. S. H. Steinberg. London:
Macmillan, 1966.

Presents what was transpiring in a given age in various parts
of the world in different fields of activity. The usual format is
six columns per time period, with the left three dealing primarily with the major powers and their relations and the right
three treating ecclesiastical history, constitutional and economic
history, and cultural life. The lack of an index is a drawback,
but the volume can be of great service to the student.

History of American Presidential Elections. Arthur Schlesinger, Jr., Fred L. Israel, and William P. Hansen, eds. New York: Chelsea House, 1971.

The most comprehensive treatment of this subject, these four volumes by forty-five experts offer an original essay on each election (averaging thirty-two pages) followed by a documentary appendix. The appendix includes party platforms, election results, correspondence, public addresses, and other related material. This will become a basic reference work for the study of American presidential elections.

International Encyclopedia of the Social Sciences. David L. Sills, ed. 16 vols. plus index. New York: Macmillan Co. and the Free Press, 1968.

Compiled by 1500 social scientists and 400 advisory editors from thirty countries, this set comprises extensive signed articles with bibliographies on topics in anthropology, economics, geography, history, law, political science, psychiatry, psychology, sociology, and statistics. It tends to be more abstract and conceptual than the older *Encyclopedia of the Social Sciences.* About a quarter of the work is composed of biographical sketches averaging 1500 words. All entries are alphabetically arranged with cross references. This set, designed to complement, not supplant, the older series, is the finest guide to the social sciences today.

Latin America and the Caribbean: A Handbook. Claudio Véliz, ed. New York: Praeger, 1968.

Another volume in Praeger's series (others include Asia, Africa, and Western Europe), it is divided into five parts: history, politics, economics, society, and the arts. It includes twenty-eight maps, fourteen pages of black and white art photographs, and a rather limited number of statistics. It is a useful ready-reference tool for information on the region.

The McGraw-Hill Encyclopedia of Russia and the Soviet Union. Michael T. Florinsky, ed. New York: McGraw-Hill, 1961.

This encyclopedia, while striving to maintain a high level of scholarship, not only lists the basic facts and figures but also offers interpretations of the principal developments. A long list of specialists contributed and initialed articles, which are fairly extensive, in government, economics, history, culture, and science. The writing styles are very readable.

The Middle East and North Africa. London: Europa Publications, 1948—. Annual.

Like the other Europa publications, this one begins with general introductory essays, treats regional organizations, includes a "Who's Who" of the region, and provides a detailed verbal and statistical portrait of each nation in the region.

The Modern Encyclopaedia of Australia and New Zealand. Sydney: Horwitz-Grahame, 1964.

This authoritative one-volume reference work includes a wealth of information on the history, people, geography, economy, and culture of Australia, New Zealand, and Papua-New Guinea. It features a chronology for the history of the countries through 1963. The appendices include a variety of tables, ranging from sports to economic production to lists of prime ministers.

The Negro Almanac. Harry A. Ploski and Roscoe C. Brown, Jr., eds. New York: Bellwether Publishing Co., 1967.

A thorough verbal and statistical documentation of the role of the Negro in the historical and contemporary United States. It includes historical documents, population statistics, economic patterns, educational and religious facts, and the many other categories of information one would expect from a specialized almanac. It is the most useful single source available on the subject.

A New Dictionary of British History. Siegfrid H. Steinberg. London: St. Martin's Press, 1963.

This one-volume work concentrates on political, constitutional, administrative, legal, ecclesiastical, and economic events at the expense of the arts and sciences. It includes countries that have at some time been a part of England or her Empire.

Wales, more closely associated with England, gets more detailed treatment than Scotland or Ireland, which are treated mostly in terms of their relations with England. Bibliographical entries are omitted. The citations are alphabetically arranged.

The Oxford Classical Dictionary. N. G. L. Hammond and H. H. Scullard, eds. Oxford: Clarendon Press, 1970.

Designed to meet the needs both of the specialist and of the general reader in all fields of ancient Greek and Roman civilization to the death of Constantine in 337. It emphasizes biography and literature without neglecting geography and bibliography. The articles are long enough to place their subjects in perspective, but brief enough to permit inclusion of the large number of references. An index of names other than the subjects of entries adds greatly to the volume's usefulness.

Reference Encyclopedia of the American Indian. Bernard Klein and Daniel Icolari, eds. New York: B. Klein and Co., 1967.

This one-volume work offers a vast array of information on the American Indian today, including government agencies, associations, reservations, tribal councils, and schools. It also has brief descriptive annotations for magazines and books dealing with the Indian; the bibliographies, arranged both by subject and alphabetically by title, are the most valuable feature for the history students. A "Who's Who" of prominent Indians and non-Indians active in Indian affairs, along the lines of *Who's Who in America*, is also of interest.

The Statesman's Year-Book: Statistical and Historical Annual of the States of the World for the Year. J. Paxton, ed. London: Macmillan and Co., 1864–. Annual.

Offers a yearly update of economic, political, and social statistics and information on international organizations, and on every country in existence during the preceding year. Data include each nation's constitution, political and governmental structure, financial basis, gross national product, court system, etc. It is independent of official approval and thus can use facts and figures that are not necessarily agreeable to certain governments. It is probably more widely used than any other yearbook save the *World Almanac.*

Webster's Geographical Dictionary. Springfield, Mass.: G. and C. Merriam Co., 1966.

A useful source for locating place names, *Webster's Geographical Dictionary* includes geographical and historical information, pronunciations, and a number of maps.

Western Europe: A Handbook. John Calmann, ed. New York: Praeger, 1967.

This extremely useful volume for the student of current history deals with twenty-seven non-Communist European nations. Part I provides historical, political, geographic, economic, and cultural information for each country. Part II treats European defense, agriculture, income, prices, immigrant labor, education, churches, and the arts on a continental basis. Part III analyzes the structures, objectives, and potentials of the institutions of Western European integration such as the EEC. The book pulls together much information that was previously scattered, and includes bibliographies for the essays in parts II and III. It is less detailed than *The Europa Yearbook,* but more interpretive.

World Almanac and Book of Facts. New York: Newspaper Enterprise Association, 1868–. Annual.

First published by the *New York World* in 1868, this has long been the standard American reference almanac. A veritable encyclopedia of current events, it is strongest in dealing with the United States, though it covers the entire world. It contains over a million facts relating to natural, social, industrial, political, financial, religious, educational, and historical subjects and statistics, plus an index.

Similar information can be found in the *Information Please Almanac* (New York: Simon and Schuster, Inc.), the *Reader's Digest Almanac and Yearbook* (Pleasantville, New York: Reader's Digest Association), and *The Official Associated Press Almanac* (Almanac Publishing Company).

B. BIBLIOGRAPHICAL AIDS

The African Experience. John N. Paden and Edward W. Soja, eds. Evanston, Ill.: Northwestern Univ. Press, 1970.

Volume IIIA (*Bibliography*) is arranged by country around a suggested course syllabus and cross referenced by author. The bibliographic entries are a useful basis for research. Volume IIIB (*Guide to Resources*) includes short essays on African studies resources, including African newspapers, journals, publishers, audio-visual aids, and bibliographies.

A Bibliography for the Study of European History, 1815-1939. Lowell J. Regatz. Ann Arbor, Michigan: Edwards Bros., 1942.

Divided into three sections: Europe as a Whole, Individual Countries, and International Relations. Chapters are subdivided by topic into social, political, economic, and cultural history, imperialism, science, government, and biography. The citations are not annotated. Three supplements have brought the work only up to 1956.

Bibliography of British History. Sources and Literature of English History . . . to 1485. Charles Gross, ed. (1915; reprint, New York: Peter Smith, 1951). *The Tudor Period, 1485-1603.* Conyers Reed, ed. (2nd ed., Oxford: Clarendon Press, 1959). *The Stuart Period, 1603-1714.* Godfrey Davies, ed. (Oxford: Clarendon Press, 1928). *The Eighteenth Century, 1714-1789.* Stanley Pargellis and D. J. Medley, eds. (Oxford: Clarendon Press, 1951).

Each of these volumes was prepared and indexed by its own author. Arranged by subject, they cover the social, cultural, political, economic, colonial, and military facets of English history. They include journal articles as well as books, making them excellent for in-depth studies of the materials up to 1789. Their aim is to include all important collections of printed sources and provide brief annotations for many of the citations. These volumes are clearly the basic source for the British history student.

A Bibliography of Modern History. John Roach, ed. Cambridge: Cambridge University Press, 1968.

Accompanies the *New Cambridge Modern History*, which omits the extensive bibliographies of the old *Cambridge Modern History*. Brief annotations for the selected 6040 entries were provided by the contributors to the *New Cambridge Modern History*. The volume emphasizes works in English published before 1961, and is probably the best general bibliography of European history from 1493 to 1945.

Bibliography of the Peoples and Cultures of Mainland Southeast Asia. John Fee Embree and Lillian Ota Dotson. New Haven: Yale Univ. Press, 1950.

The essential bibliography for Burma, Indochina, and Thailand. It notes 12,000 books and articles in Western languages about archaeology, ethnology, cultural history, social organization, and law. It is arranged by country and topic, but has only occasional brief annotations.

China: A Critical Bibliography. Charles O. Hucker. Tuscon: Univ. of Arizona Press, 1962.

This superb bibliography arranges 2285 usefully annotated citations by topic, includes a detailed table of contents to lead the student directly to his area, and also features an author index. Within each subject grouping, entries are arranged in the order in which Hucker would recommend them to an introductory college student. The citations stress books and articles published in English since 1940.

China in Western Literature: A Continuation of Cordier's "Bibliotheca Sinica." T'ung-li Yüan. New Haven: Yale Univ. Press, 1958.

An indispensable list of almost all books concerning China published in English, French, and German between 1921 and 1957. It supplements the original *Bibliotheca Sinica* by Henri Cordier, a four-volume work completed in 1908 and updated in 1924, which is the basic bibliography of Western language books and articles on China. The new volume is arranged topically and includes a name index. This is *the* starting point for a study of China before 1957.

Contemporary China: A Research Guide. Peter Berton and Eugene Wu. Stanford: The Hoover Institute on War, Revolution, and Peace, 1967.

Treats post-1945 Taiwan and post-1949 Mainland China, stressing the social sciences and humanities. The entries are well annotated, and it has useful author-title and subject indexes. Its purpose is to facilitate research on contemporary China by providing descriptions of the most important bibliographical and reference works, selected documentary compilations, and listings of series, dissertations, and theses. It deals mainly in English, Chinese, Japanese, and Russian-language publications.

Dissertations in History: An Index to Dissertations Completed in History Departments of United States and Canadian Universities, 1873-1960. Warren F. Kuehl. Lexington: Univ. of Kentucky Press, 1965.

Pulls together all doctoral dissertations in the field of history, arranges them alphabetically by the author's name, and includes a subject index. Each entry includes the title, university, and date. The index indicates which topics are neglected, which are overworked, and offers a multitude of ideas. Beginning in 1961, *Dissertations Abstracts* added a topical index, so the student is now able to find dissertation titles for any year since 1873.

A Guide to Archives and Manuscripts in the United States. Phillip M. Hamer, ed. New Haven: Yale Univ. Press, 1961.

Arranges by state and city over 7600 collections of personal papers in 1300 depositories throughout the United States, Puerto Rico, and the Canal Zone. It describes major holdings, notes published information on individual collections, and includes an index to depositories, proper names, and subjects. For each depository there is generally a broad statement of its particular field of interest and an indication of the size of its holdings. Groups of papers regarded as being of special interest

are then specifically mentioned, facilitating rapid identification
of the appropriate collection.

Guide to Historical Literature. American Historical Association.
New York: Macmillan, 1961.

   "Designed to furnish directions to the best means of gaining a broader knowledge of history," this is an admirable
starting place for the student preparing a paper. It is divided
into nine sections: Introduction and General History, Historical
Beginnings, The Middle Period in Eurasia and North Africa, Asia
Since Early Times, Modern Europe, The Americas, Africa,
Australasia and Oceania, and The World in Recent Times. Each
section offers an annotated selection of the basic materials
arranged by form (such as bibliographies, general histories,
periodicals, reference works). An emphasis on English-language
materials and a detailed index add to the book's usefulness. This
is the best source for general world history.

A Guide to Latin American Studies. Martin Sable. UCLA: Latin
American Center, 1967.

   These two volumes include roughly 5000 annotations of
selected works in all areas relating to Latin America. They offer
guidance to basic and advanced textbooks, standard reference
sources, conference proceedings, periodicals, documents, and
pamphlet material. The works are arranged alphabetically by
broad subject divisions. The guide includes author and subject
indexes. It extends Robin Humphrey's *Latin American History*
by including Portuguese and Spanish-language works (as well as
a few in other languages), and most notably by the thorough
and very valuable annotations. This is a truly excellent source.

Guide to Reference Books. Constance M. Winchell, ed. Chicago:
American Library Association, 1967.

   The most comprehensive of all guides of this type, the
Guide to Reference Books was first published in 1902 and
through eight editions has kept conspicuously up to date. The
latest edition divides 7500 titles into five categories: general
reference works, humanities, social sciences, history and area
studies, and the pure and applied sciences. The history and area

studies section is arranged by geographical area (General, Americas, Europe, Africa, Asia, Australia and New Zealand, Oceanica, and the Arctic and Antarctic) and then lists countries alphabetically. French sources, for example, are subdivided into seven categories of bibliography, dictionaries and handbooks, atlases, general histories, and Paris. All entries are annotated, but usually only with a sentence or two. A lengthy index includes subject, author, and title citations.

Guide to Russian Reference Books. Karol Maichal. ed. by J. S. G. Simmons. Stanford: The Hoover Institute on War, Revolution, and Peace, 1962—.

The first general guide to Russian bibliographies and reference books. It selectively covers reference works listing materials from the eleventh century to 1960, and deals only with Russian and Western European language materials. The first two volumes deal extensively with bibliographies, then with encyclopedias, biographical dictionaries, handbooks, and other source materials. Volume five treats science and technology, while volumes three, four, and six have not yet appeared. The annotations are excellent.

Guide to the Diplomatic History of the United States, 1775-1921. Samuel Flagg Bemis and Grace Gardner Griffin. Washington, D.C.: Government Printing Office, 1935.

The best source extant for facts on American diplomatic history up to 1921. Part one guides the reader chronologically toward books, journals, chapters of books, manuscript collections, and maps. Part two notes the best government sources and explains how to locate them. The book is in the form of a bibliographical essay. Indexes to collections of personal papers and to authors are helpful.

A Guide to the Study of Medieval History. Louis J. Paetow, ed. Dana C. Munro and Gray C. Boyce, eds., rev. ed. New York: F. S. Crofts and Co., 1931.

This comprehensive, scholarly, and critical guide is still the best in its field, even though outdated. Part one covers bibliographical works, reference materials, auxiliaries to the study of medieval history, general modern historical works, and large collections of original sources. Part two concerns the general history of the Middle Ages, and part three deals with medieval culture. Both grew out of a medieval history course outline. Occasional critical notes have been inserted.

A Guide to the Study of the United States of America: Representative Books Reflecting the Development of American Life and Thought. Roy P. Basler, Donald R. Mugridge, and Blanche P. McCrum. Washington, D. C.: Government Printing Office, 1960.

This massive guide is divided into thirty-two chapters and includes some 6400 well-annotated items published before 1958. Topics include general, diplomatic, intellectual, military, and local history. The useful index includes authors, titles, and subjects. The object of the volume is to offer a panorama of American life, past and present, relating to subjects as divergent as art and public health. The annotations are highly useful as summaries of the views of the various authors.

Harvard Guide to American History. Oscar Handlin, Arthur Schlesinger, Sr., Samuel Eliot Morison, Frederick Merk, Arthur Schlesinger, Jr., and Paul Buck. Cambridge: Harvard Univ. Press, Belknap Press, 1954.

Six distinguished Harvard professors collaborated on this excellent guide to the literature of American history. Seeking to include both old and new books of value and distinction, and at the same time preserve a balance between general works and more specialized monographs, they have provided a classic reference work that includes a very good index to authors, titles, and subjects. It is divided into six parts: Status, Methods, and Presentation; Materials and Tools; Colonial History and the Revolution; National Growth, 1789-1865; The Rise of Modern America; and America in the Twentieth Century. Its biggest shortcoming is that 1950 is the last year from which publications were accepted. It badly needs updating.

Historical Bibliographies: A Systematic and Annotated Guide. Edith M. Coulter and Melanie Gerstenfeld, eds. New York: Russell and Russell, 1965.

Strikes a happy medium between manuals so general as to be of little practical service and others which are of use to specialists only. It can give the student a perspective on historical literature and guidance through it. The bibliographies are arranged by period, country, and episode, and each entry has a brief, uncritical descriptive annotation. A helpful author and subject index is provided.

Interpreting and Teaching American History. William H. Cartwright and Richard L. Watson, eds. Washington, D.C.: National Council for the Social Studies, 1961. (31st NCSS Yearbook).

Three-fourths of this volume consists of good introductory bibliographical essays on the various periods of American history. Though far from comprehensive, the essays are written by first-rank historians and note major trends in the historiography of each period and describe the major works involved.

Japan and Korea: A Critical Bibliography. Bernard S. Silberman. Tuscon: Univ. of Arizona Press, 1962.

Like its counterpart on Chinese history, this fine bibliography utilizes a topical arrangement within which authoritativeness and availability determine the order of listing. The detailed table of contents, author index, and fine brief annotations to the 1933 entries make this an excellent beginning point for a paper on the area.

Latin American History: A Guide to the Literature in English. Robin Arthur Humphreys. London: Oxford Univ. Press, 1958.

Provides annotations for 2089 books and periodical articles in the areas of economic, political, and sociological history. Issued under the auspices of the Royal Institute of International Affairs, it is organized by topic, period, and geographical area. There are occasional brief but helpful annotations. It includes a list of periodicals cited, a biographical index, and an index of authors, editors, and translators.

List of Doctoral Dissertations in History in Progress in the United States. Washington, D. C.: American Historical Association, 1909—.

This triennial list, arranged by field of history, permits one to keep abreast of the latest graduate research. It includes author and topic indexes, a list of universities represented, and a detailed topical table of contents. Each citation notes a title, author, and university.

National Union Catalogue of Manuscripts. Washington, D.C.: Library of Congress, 1962—.

A continuing publication, *NUCMC* seeks ultimately to catalogue all manuscript collections with over fifty items in the United States. To date, 723 repositories with 23,053 collections have been described. The indexed entries include the collection title, physical description, location, scope, and content, and information on access and literary rights.

The Negro in America: A Bibliography. Mary L. Fisher. Cambridge: Harvard Univ. Press, 1970.

A thorough bibliography of both books and articles dealing with all aspects of black history in the United States. Though it is not annotated, the thorough coverage given such topics as urban problems, education, politics, music, and many others will lead the student directly to specific works of value to him. It is much more inclusive than *The Negro in the United States* and "encompasses the clinical, empirical, prescriptive, and polemic, the scholarly and the journalistic" (p. xix). This is the basic bibliography for the student of American Negro history.

The Negro in the United States: A Selected Bibliography Dorothy B. Porter. Washington, D.C.: Government Printing Office, 1970.

The emphasis in this selected list is on recent monographs in the Library of Congress. They are arranged alphabetically by author under broad subject headings that reveal the Negro's role in numerous aspects of American life, culture, and history

Topics covered include the urban Negro, race relations, discriminatory practices, education, religion, social conditions, and biographical works. Occasionally brief annotations are included, and the book provides an index of names and subjects.

Oriental and Asian Bibliography: An Introduction with Some Reference to Africa. J. D. Pearson. London: Crosby Lockwood and Son, 1966.

Approaches Oriental and Asian bibliography as a whole, and is therefore primarily concerned with institutions, books, and libraries relating to all or most of the continent. Part one deals with institutions producing literature. Part two cites the European materials relating to Asia and includes catalogs and indexes. Part three lists libraries and archives storing the literature. The work includes an author index, and is generally written in prose form.

Russia and the Soviet Union: A Bibliographic Guide to Western-Language Publications. Paul L. Horecky, ed. Chicago: Univ. of Chicago Press, 1965.

An accurately and informatively annotated companion to Horecky's volume on Russian-language publications. It is divided into nine major sections: general reference aids and bibliographies, general descriptive works, the land, the people, the nation's history, the state, the economic and social structure, and intellectual and cultural life. The thirty-one scholars involved in the project have rigorously selected the best sources available and produced an excellent source for students of Russia.

A Select Bibliography: Asia, Africa, Eastern Europe, and Latin America. New York: American Universities Field Staff, Inc., 1960.

Lists some 6000 current books and academic journal articles available for college study and general reading. Most entries have brief descriptive and analytic annotations of considerable value, particularly to the novice. They are arranged by regional and cultural sections within each major geographic area, and are subdivided by subject or chronology. It includes both subject and author indexes. It is unusual among bibliographies in that it makes a systematic qualitative distinction between first choice, labeled A, and second choice, labeled B, for about half the entries.

A Select List of Books on European History, 1815-1914. L. C. Bullock and A. J. P. Taylor. Oxford: Clarendon Press, 1957.

A brief, selective bibliography of secondary works in English and common Western European languages. It is designed to be a practical book list, not an exercise in academic or bibliographical scholarship. Clearly organized, it provides a simple jumping-off point for the beginning student looking for the basic books. There are no annotations.

Select List of Books on the Orient. W. A. C. H. Dobson, ed. Oxford: Clarendon Press, 1955.

A brief introduction to the best of the literature, mostly in English, about Asia. It is divided into sections on Ancient Egypt and the Ancient Near East and Middle East, Islam, India and Further India, and the Far East. It treats only 870 reliable and readable books, and is arranged to facilitate the novice's research.

Slavic Europe: A Selected Bibliography in the Western European Languages. R. J. Kerner. Cambridge: Harvard Univ. Press 1918.

Seeks to guide Western Europeans and Americans to an understanding of a neglected area of Europe. Dividing the topic into Slavs, Russians, Poles, German Slavs, Bohemians, Slovaks, and Southern Slavs, it treats the language, literature, and history of each. The obvious major drawback is that it is over fifty years out-of-date, despite a 1969 reissue by Russell and Russell of New York.

Les Sources du travail bibliographique. Louise-Noëlle Malclès, ed. Geneva: E. Droz, 1950-58.

Designed as a textbook and guide, this three-volume French-language work has considerable introductory material. It emphasizes French and European works of the past twenty-five years, though it includes basic earlier works. The second volume offers the most assistance to the undergraduate student, including periodicals, encyclopedias, dictionaries, and bibliographies in humanities and social sciences.

Writings on British History. London: J. C. Cape, 1937–.

This series treats books about Great Britain prior to 1914, and includes some seventeen volumes to date. It is arranged by year of publication, which is a trifle awkward. A comprehensive bibliography emphasizing English-language materials, it arranges entries under general works and periods of English history. The lack of annotations is a drawback, though there is compensation in references to reviews. There is an author-subject index in each volume.

C. GUIDES TO PERIODICAL LITERATURE

America: History and Life: A Guide to Periodical Literature. Eric H. Boehm, ed. Santa Barbara: Clio Press for the American Bibliographical Center, 1964–. Quarterly.

An outstanding new guide to periodical literature, *America: History and Life* should be the first source for the student seeking articles on United States and Canadian history. It is divided into six sections: North America, Canada, United States to 1945, United States since 1945, regional, state, and local history, and historiography and methodology. The abstracts identify the author, give the full title of the article and periodical, the volume number, date, and pages, and provide commentary averaging about 150 words. The speed with which articles are cited in the guide after their publication further enhances this quarterly's great value. *Historical Abstracts* provides a similar service for world history.

American Newspapers, 1821-1936: A Union List of Files Available in the United States and Canada. Winifred Gregory, ed. New York: H. W. Wilson, 1937.

Provides the student with an authoritative, easily understandable means of locating newspapers. The book is arranged alphabetically by state or province and city. Newspapers are alphabetically listed under each city, and each entry includes the name, frequency of publication, dates, title changes, and names of libraries holding files, with dates held. This is the basic source for the student wishing to utilize newspapers for the period before 1936.

Ayer Directory of Newspapers, Magazines, and Trade Publications. Leonard Bray, ed. Philadelphia: Ayer Press, 1869–. Annual.

The *Ayer Directory* is designed "to provide facts about newspapers and magazines, and authoritative information concerning the states, cities, towns, and marketing areas in which these publications are issued and circulate." It is "the recognized key to nearly every kind of publication issued in the United States and Canada. It is widely used as the basic authority by people in business, industry, education, agriculture, religion, government, and advertising" (p. iv).

For each publication it lists publication frequency, founding date, size, subscription rate, circulation, and political preference. For each state, province, or country (Bermuda, Panama, and the Philippines) it provides information about population, agriculture, topography, fisheries, forests, manufactures, minerals, and miscellany. It also includes a detailed map of each state, province, or nation and a list of every town over 2500. The nature of the *Ayer Directory* makes it particularly valuable for the student seeking some idea of the political leaning and potential influence of a publication.

Book Review Digest. New York: H. W. Wilson Co., 1905–.

An indexed monthly reference to selected book reviews drawn from about seventy-five popular English and American periodicals. It is arranged by author and has title and subject indexes. Each issue covers from 300 to 400 titles, and presents excerpts from several reviews and a list of those not excerpted. It is a good tool for locating reviews, but the student should be aware that it does not cite all possible reviews.

Editor and Publisher International Yearbook. New York: Editor and Publisher, 1920—. Annual.

The finest guide to the world's press. In it are listed current daily newspapers in the United States, Canada, Latin America, Europe, Australasia, Africa, the Near and Middle East, and Asia. In addition, weeklies in the United States, American Negro newspapers, special service dailies, and college, professional, and business papers are noted. Special features include groupings of American dailies under common ownership, lists of foreign press correspondents in the United States, and a feature news and picture syndicate directory.

Half a Century of Soviet Serials, 1917-1968: A Bibliography and Union List of Serials Published in the U.S.S.R. Rudolf Smits. Washington, D.C.: Government Printing Office, 1968.

This extensive (29,761 entries with over 28,000 cross references) two-volume work includes all known serial publications to appear in the Soviet Union (except in Oriental Languages) since 1917. Titles are followed by place of publication, year publication began, the name of issuing body, frequency of publication, and miscellaneous other helpful remarks. Of particular usefulness, each entry notes which American and Canadian libraries possess files of that periodical. Much of the writing is in Russian.

Historical Abstracts, 1775-1945: Bibliography of the World's Periodical Literature. Eric H. Boehm, ed. Santa Barbara: Clio Press with the International Social Science Institute, 1955—. Quarterly.

Covers all areas of modern history for the period cited. It is divided into three major sections: (1) General (general bibliography, methodology and research methods, historiography, philosophy and interpretation of history, archives, libraries and institutions, meetings, and pedagogy; (2) Topics (international relations, wars and military history, economic history, social and cultural history, religion and churches, sciences and technology); and (3) Area or Country (Africa, Asia and the Pacific, Latin America, North America, Europe, and Russia).

Each signed abstract includes the author's full name, the article's title, the periodical, volume number, date, pages, and excellent commentary. Annual subject-name indexes are supplemented by five-year indexes. This is the outstanding world-history analogue to *America: History and Life.*

Index to Latin American Periodical Literature, 1929-1960. Pan American Union. Boston: G. K. Hall and Co., 1962.

An outstanding index to the periodical literature of Latin American history. It includes articles from over 3000 different periodicals, as indexed at the Columbus Memorial Library of the Pan American Union. The eight massive volumes include some 250,000 entries of authors, subjects, and other secondary entries in the form of photographs of the library's catalog cards. Thus there are no annotations. Two supplementary volumes bring the series through 1965.

International Guide to Medieval Studies: A Quarterly Index to Periodical Literature. Darien, Conn.: American Bibliographical Service, 1961 –.

One of a number of new serials dealing with studies of the Middle Ages. It lists articles alphabetically by author and also cites full-length reviews of recent medieval publications. Cumulative author and subject indexes are useful.

Another similar publication is the semi-annual *International Medieval Bibliography* issued by the University of Minnesota's History Department since 1967. Arranged by subject, it cites periodical articles from 160 journals and includes indexes of authors and personal and place names.

Newspapers on Microfilm. George A. Schwegmann, Jr. Washington, D.C.: Library of Congress, 1967.

The United States (broken down by state), Canada, and 136 foreign countries are represented in this listing. The vast majority of the approximately 21,700 entries are drawn from the United States and its possessions, though over 4600 foreign newspapers are included. As microfilms become more common and libraries enlarge their collections, this guide will become increasingly valuable.

New York Times Index. New York: New York Times, 1913—.

The major reference source for an accurate chronological list of important events. It presents an extensive and detailed look at the world news as reported by the *New York Times*, a paper offering unmatched world and financial coverage. The *Index* cites the date, page, and column with many cross references and serves as a reference for material in other newspapers as well. One of the features that students find most attractive is the brief synopsis under each entry, which frequently makes reference to the newspaper itself unnecessary. The *Index* has been published semimonthly with annual cumulations since 1930. R. R. Bowker Co., New York, is now publishing in book form the indexes since the paper's 1851 founding; they are presently available only on microfilm.

Poole's Index to Periodical Literature, 1802-1907. Boston: Houghton Mifflin, 1882-1908.

This seven-volume guide is invaluable because it is the only index to pre-1890 periodicals. It should be used in concert with *Poole's Index, Date and Key Volume*, which lists the 479 periodicals indexed and provides dates for the otherwise mystifying volume numbers. The value of the index is increasing greatly, for University Microfilms is filming the British and American periodicals listed in it, and thus the student will be readily able to utilize the 590,000 articles indexed, and a whole century of important literature will become easily accessible.

Reader's Guide to Periodical Literature. New York: H. W. Wilson Co., 1905—.

One of the most valuable reference works in the library, the *Reader's Guide* indexes (but does not annotate) articles from about 135 popular American journals, including a few of scholarly quality. It provides a detailed alphabetical key to magazine articles, their authors, where and when the articles were published, and their page references. It appears biweekly with annual cumulations, and has been extended back to 1890 to fill the gap left by *Poole's Index*. This is a basic source for twentieth-century American history.

Social Sciences and Humanities Index. New York: H. W. Wilson Co., 1907—.

This quarterly index is a fine starting point for the history student. It covers 215 scholarly journals in history, archaeology, economics, literature, political science, sociology, religion, and other areas. Though it treats only English-language publications, the nature of the periodicals included makes it a better source than the more popular *Reader's Guide.* It includes an author-subject index.

Ulrich's International Periodicals Directory. New York: R. R. Bowker, 1971-72.

Ulrich's two-volume guide to current domestic and foreign periodicals is arranged by subject and indexed by title and subject. In addition to entries for some 50,000 current periodicals, it has lists of new and ceased titles since the last edition. It provides complete data on name, publisher, dates, frequency, and where possible, circulation and other information. This is the basic guide to the world's current periodicals.

Union List of Latin American Newspapers in Libraries in the United States. Arthur E. Gropp. Washington, D.C.: Department of Cultural Affairs, Pan American Union, 1953.

Cites over 5000 titles in fifty-six libraries. They are arranged alphabetically by country of origin, then by city and title. The entries include title, frequency, dates of origin and cessation, and language.

Union List of Serials in Libraries of the United States and Canada. Edna Brown Titus. New York: H. W. Wilson Co., 1965.

This five-volume work is probably the finest example of a union list. The third edition lists locations for 157,000 journals in 956 Canadian and American libraries. Each title is followed by its dates of publication and then by a list of all libraries holding issues of the periodical and the issues held. This extremely valuable reference work is kept up to date by *New Serials Titles,* a monthly supplement.

Biographical Directories and Related Works. Robert B. Slocum. Detroit: Gale Research Co., 1967.

This guide is over 1000 pages long and lists 4829 different sources of biographical information with brief annotations. It includes author, title, and subject indexes, and is the best source to check to see if your topic has more specific biographical aids available.

Biographical Directory of the American Congress, 1774-1971. Washington, D.C.: Government Printing Office, 1971.

This handy reference tool for the political historian is the latest edition of a work dating from 1859. It includes a listing of executive officers for each administration, delegates to the Continental Congress, and a chronological listing of the senators and representatives of each Congress since 1789. Over three-fourths of the book is made up of over 10,800 biographical sketches of everyone ever to serve in Congress. The alphabetically arranged sketches average about 200 words and provide the pertinent information about their subjects' lives and careers.

Biographical Sources for the United States. Jane Kline. Washington, D.C.: Government Printing Office, 1961

A brief directory of the various biographical guides available for the study of living Americans. It is arranged in three sections: general, regions and states, and special and professional groups. This annotated list includes a subject and title index.

Biography Index. New York: H. W. Wilson Co., 1947–. Quarterly.

Enables the student to locate the latest biographical information on living and deceased figures of at least moderate importance. It cites material in periodicals, "individual and collective biographies . . . obituaries, collections of letters, diaries, memoirs, bibliographies, and incidental biographical material in otherwise non-biographical books" (p. v). The index, subdivided by profession or occupation, is designed for both scholarly and general use. Each entry includes dates, profession,

Union Lists of Serials. Ruth S. Freitag, ed. Washington, D.C.: Government Printing Office, 1964.

Lists world publications that indicate the location of serials in more than one library. The arrangement of entries is geographical, then alphabetical within each section. The volume includes geographical, name, and subject indexes. There are brief annotations for each of the 1218 lists recorded.

Willing's European Press Guide. New York: R. R. Bowker, 1968.

Includes 50,000 newspapers, periodicals, and annuals from eleven Western European countries. They are arranged and cross-referenced by subject under more than 180 headings. Each entry includes name, address, publisher, frequency, and price. There are subject indexes in English, French, German, and Italian; a title index would be useful. A companion volume, *Willing's Press Guide*, has provided a similar service for the United Kingdom since 1874.

D. BIOGRAPHICAL REFERENCES

The Almanac of American Politics. Michael Barone, Grant Ujifusa, and Douglas Matthews, eds. Boston: Gambit, 1972.

Provides better biographical data than the *Congressional Directory*. It includes a photo, biography and career, committee assignments, group ratings (such as ADA, COPE), key votes, and recent election results for each senator and congressman. It also places each figure in context by detailing the nature of his constituency, including population, federal outlays and tax burden, the district's overall political makeup, and the ethnic composition of the voters. It is an invaluable reference tool for contemporary politics.

Biographical Dictionary of Republican China. Howard L. Boorman, ed. 4 vols. New York: Columbia University Press, 1967.

Some 600 lengthy articles treat the leaders of Republican China from 1911 to 1949. There is no effort to list those who became prominent following the move to Taiwan, but this is the basic source for information about most of today's older leaders.

nationality, location of the biography, and presence or absence of illustration. This publication is a vital source for any student seeking the most up-to-date material on a historical or contemporary figure.

Concise Dictionary of American Biography. Joseph G. E. Hopkins, managing ed., New York: Charles Scribner's Sons, 1964.

Condenses all 14,870 biographies from the *Dictionary of American Biography* to about one-fourteenth their length and includes the essential facts in one volume for quick reference.

Current Biography. New York, H. W. Wilson Co., 1940–. Monthly.

Current Biography supplies unbiased, well-written sketches of contemporary personalities in about forty different professional fields. The articles generally include a photograph, name (with pronunciation, if difficult), birth date, occupation, reason for prominence, address, and references to sources of further information. The articles average over two double-columned pages in length. Each issue includes obituary notices with reference to the last full-length article on the deceased. The 325 or so personalities covered are classified by profession at the end of the volume, which also includes an index for the current decade.

Dictionary of American Biography. American Council of Learned Societies. 20 vols. plus index. New York: Charles Scribner's Sons, 1928-37. *Supplement One* (1944). *Supplement Two* (1958).

Patterned after Britain's *Dictionary of National Biography* this is *the* outstanding source for detailed information on 14,870 prominent Americans who died before 1940. The extensive, colorfully written articles, when possible based on primary sources, include ancestry, parentage, education, achievements, and a useful bibliography. The handy index volume is subdivided into biographees, biographers, birthplaces, schools attended, occupations, and subjects. This is the most famous and most reliable of all American biographical dictionaries. It has been condensed into the *Concise Dictionary of American Biography.*

Dictionary of Canadian Biography. Toronto: University of Toronto Press, 1966–. 20 vols. planned.

The Canadian equivalent of the *Dictionary of National Biography.* Unlike it, *DCB* treats the subjects according to historical period, with one's death date determining his place in the series. Within each chronological volume the entries appear chronologically. This permits an understanding of each figure in relation to the development of Canada and at the same time facilitates revision of each volume independently of the others. Thus far volumes I (to 1700) and II (1700-1740) have appeared, with almost 1200 entries varying in length from 200 to 10,000 words.

The Macmillan Dictionary of Canadian Biography (Toronto: Macmillan, 1963) provides a one-volume treatment that will serve while the multi-volume *DCB* is being compiled.

Dictionary of National Biography. Leslie Stephen and Sidney Lee, eds. 22 vols. London: Smith, Elder, 1885-1901.

The original great biographical reference work in the English-speaking world, and still the finest source for biographical information on deceased personages of Great Britain, Ireland, and the British colonies. The original twenty-two volumes included 29,120 articles, and have been updated through 1950 by six supplemental volumes. The articles vary greatly in length, ranging from many pages to less than a column, depending on the significance of the subject. The portraits are objective, scholarly, and highly readable. This should be the first source consulted for English biography.

Dictionnaire de biographie française. Paris: Letouzey et Ané, 1932–.

An enormous undertaking, the *Dictionnaire de biographie française* issues several softcover sections each year; six of them form a hardbound volume. Through 1971 some thirteen volumes have appeared, with only A-E covered. The articles tend to be shorter than in the *DNB,* but all are signed and most have bibliographies. The number of Frenchmen, colonists, and people of importance to France will be exhaustive by the time the work is completed some time in the distant future. The writing is, of course, in French.

Directory of American Scholars. New York: R. R. Bowker Co., 1969.

This four-volume set provides biographical information on some 33,500 scholars in history, English, foreign languages, philosophy, religion, and law. Volume I treats 9500 historians, providing name, birthdate and place, citizenship, date of marriage, children, fields of specialization, education, position, military service, society membership, research, publications, and address. Inclusion in the book requires a historian to have a more than local reputation and to have achieved stature in scholarly work.

International Who's Who. London: Europa Publications, 1935–. Annual.

Includes over 10,000 sketches based on replies to questionnaires sent to the subjects. It provides name, title, dates, nationality, education, profession, career, achievements, publications, and address in the standard *Who's Who* format.

The Japan Biographical Encyclopedia and Who's Who. Tokyo: The Rengo Press, 1964-65.

Lists 15,200 figures and includes special features such as a glossary, lists of leading companies and officers, emperors, cabinets, and marriage relationships. The style is far less formal than most *Who's Who* volumes, but there are less data on each entry.

The National Cyclopedia of American Biography. Raymond D. McGill, ed. New York: James T. White and Co., 1892–. Current Volumes, A–L, 1930–. Permanent Volumes 1-54, 1892–.

Provides the best source of information on living persons (current volumes have much fuller citations than *Who's Who in America*) and a more likely source for the deceased than the

Dictionary of American Biography, which provides more commentary and information on the smaller number of figures it includes. The *National Cyclopedia* sketches over 52,000 biographies ranging in length from a paragraph to an extended essay, each accompanied by a photograph. The initially confusing arrangement is roughly chronological rather than alphabetical, so the index volumes are essential. As individuals die, they are removed from the current volume and added to the latest permanent volume.

Neue deutsche Biographie. ed. by the Historical Commission at the Bavarian Academy of Sciences. Berlin: Dunker & Humblot, 1953–.

A new edition to update the massive 56-volume *Allgemeine deutsche Biographie* completed in 1912, the *Neue deutsche Biographie* will include prominent Germans, Austrians, and Swiss who died through 1952. A more modest undertaking than its predecessor, the proposed twelve-volume work has signed articles with bibliographies along the lines of the *DNB* and *DAB*, and is thoroughly cross-referenced with the *Allgemeine deutsche Biographie.*

The New York Times Obituaries Index, 1858-1968. New York: New York Times, 1970.

Not only does this list all obituaries from the *Times* for 110 years, but it guides the reader right to the page with all the details. There are a total of over 353,000 names included.

Political Africa: A Who's Who of Personalities and Parties. Ronald Segal, ed. London: Stevens and Sons, 1961.

This directory of a region in political turmoil was dated before it was even off the press, but still provides a good source of biographical information about the African leadership of the recent past. It is more informal than the standard *Who's Who* in its approach and admittedly reflects the editor's opinion, but not at the price of accuracy. In addition to the biographies, it includes a nation-by-nation analysis of political parties. For recently updated, formal biographical information, see *Africa South of the Sahara.*

Webster's Biographical Dictionary. Springfield, Mass.: G. and C. Merriam Co., 1943. Updated annually.

A superb collection of biographical notes, *Webster's Biographical Dictionary* is not limited by historical period, nationality, race, religion, or occupation—in short, it seeks to provide a complete list of the most important personages in world history. Aimed at the English-speaking public, it does stress British and American names, however. Citations include name (with pronunciation), dates, occupation, birthplace, and achievements. Extensive tables at the end of the book provide a handy listing of political leaders throughout the world, dating back as far as they were recorded. This is an excellent starting point for the student lacking any information on the person he is investigating; there are over 40,000 citations.

Who's Who. London: A. and C. Black, 1849—.

The British pioneer of the many *Who's Who's* now available for almost any country or field. It did not begin providing biographical sketches until 1897, but since has been the standard reference work for prominent figures in many fields, including a few non-British subjects of exceptional importance. It cites name, birthdate and place, parents, family, education, career, associations, publications, and addresses of over 20,000 figures. It is up to date and reliable—each subject has an opportunity to revise his entry. Particularly helpful for Americans is a complete list of abbreviations, enabling the student to analyze the often confusing series of initials following many names.

Who's Who in America. Chicago: A. N. Marquis Co., 1899—. Biennial.

Patterned after the British *Who's Who*, this work cites the best-known figures in all field of endeavor. There are over 66,000 sketches in the latest edition. It includes name, birthplace and date, residence, parentage, education, family, career, achievements, publications, and associations.

The volume is supplemented by regional *Who's Who's* (East, Midwest, West, and South) that average 14,000 names, most not included in the national volume.

Who's Who in American Politics. Paul A. Theis and Edmund L. Henshaw, Jr., eds. New York: R. R. Bowker Co., 1971.

First published to cover the 1967-68 period, this is a biographical directory of 15,800 political leaders in the United States. It is a thorough and authoritative publication bearing the credentials of both major political parties. The biographical material was gathered by questionnaire.

Who's Who in Communist China. Hong Kong: Union Research Institute, 1969. 2 vols.

Somewhat less formal than the standard *Who's Who*, this volume lists over 3000 leading figures from party, government, military, and other areas of Chinese society.

Who's Who in France: Dictionnaire biographique. Paris: J. Lafitte, 1953–. Biennial.

The 1971-72 edition of this French-language volume includes almost 21,000 biographical sketches using the standard *Who's Who* format. It also includes guides to French companies, medals, political leaders, and other general information.

Who's Who in Germany. H. G. Kliemann and Stephen S. Taylor, eds. Munich: R. Oldenbourg, 1956–.

This two-volume English-language biographical dictionary lists some 12,000 figures in the standard *Who's Who* format.

Who's Who in History. New York: Barnes and Noble, 1960-69.

This four-volume work recasts much of Britain's monumental *DNB* into chronological time periods, with each volume's entries appearing chronologically rather than alphabetically (an index is provided). The four volumes, divided at 1485, 1603, and 1714, and concluding in 1789, include some portraits and some family trees and far fewer ecclesiastical figures than are found in the *DNB*. The essay form is used rather than *Who's Who* style.

Who's Who in Latin America. Ronald Hilton, ed. Stanford: Stanford Univ. Press, 1945-51.

Following the format of most *Who's Who* directories, *Who's Who in Latin America* limits its sketches to recitals of the pertinent facts about the citizens of Latin American nations. Unlike the alphabetically arranged one-volume earlier editions, the third edition is arranged in seven slim volumes according to geography. It has been expanded to some 8000 entries and represents the first source of information on figures prominent in most fields of endeavor in Latin America.

Who's Who in the U.S.S.R. New York: Scarecrow Press, 1965-66.

The Soviet Union's biographical directory includes about 5000 prominent personalities and is written in English.

Who Was When? A Dictionary of Contemporaries. Miriam Allen de Ford. New York: H. W. Wilson Co., 1950.

A unique volume, *Who Was When?* has taken the most important births and deaths of each year from 500 B.C. to A.D. 1949 and listed them in ten columns according to their major field of achievement. There are no annotations.

Who Was Who in America. Chicago: Marquis-Who's Who, Inc. *Historical Volume, 1607-1897* (1963). Vol. I, *1897-1942* (1943). Vol. II, *1943-1950* (1950). Vol. III, *1951-1960* (1960). Vol. IV, *1961-1968* (1968).

These volumes treat the public figures who died during the time span covered, mainly utilizing old *Who's Who* sketches (except for the *Historical Volume*). They are useful to the historian seeking more detailed information than a more general source like *Webster's Biographical Dictionary* offers on people not prominent enough for inclusion in the *National Cyclopedia* or the *DAB*.

E. ATLASES AND STATISTICAL VOLUMES

American Heritage Pictorial Atlas of United States History. New York: McGraw-Hill Book Co., 1966.

American Heritage's superb atlas includes 210 maps, portfolios of pictorial maps (Revolutionary War battles, Civil War battles, nineteenth-century cities, and U. S. National Parks), and a lively text by several historians. The maps treat all aspects of American history—political, economic, social, cultural, and geographic. This atlas is an up-to-date and highly useful aid to the study of United States history.

Annual Abstract of Statistics. Central Statistical Office, Great Britain. London: H. M. Stationery Office, 1854—. Annual.

The British analogue to *Statistical Abstract of the United States*, providing extensive statistics on population, society, education, trade, labor, transportation, finance, business, and industry. Like its American counterpart it also has a historical edition, the *Abstract of British Historical Statistics* (1962), which is useful to its 1938 cut-off date. This is clearly the basic source for any statistical information about the United Kingdom.

Atlas of World History. Robert R. Palmer, ed. New York: Rand McNally and Co., 1957.

This short atlas provides 125 maps (75 in color) of world history, with an emphasis on nineteenth and twentieth century European and American development. Economic and social history are depicted along with the standard political maps. The extensive text, which explains the maps, makes this atlas particularly useful.

Historical Statistics of Canada. M. C. Urquhart and K. A. H. Buckley, eds. Toronto: Macmillan, 1965.

This thorough survey of Canadian economic, social, and political history through statistics deals in depth with the period from Confederation to 1960. Accompanying each section is a lengthy essay introduction designed to obviate any other background sources. This is the basic source for Canadian statistical history.

Historical Statistics of the United States, Colonial Times to 1957. Washington, D.C.: Government Printing Office, 1960. *Continuation to 1962,* 1965.

The historical supplement to the *Statistical Abstract of the United States*, this volume contains over 8000 statistical studies grouped mostly into yearly periods. It covers economic and social developments from 1610 to 1962 and includes definitions of terms and descriptive text. Source notes provide a guide for students who wish to read the original published sources for further reference and data. It contains a complete subject index alphabetically arranged.

Shepherd's Historical Atlas. William R. Shepherd. 9th ed. New York: Barnes and Noble, 1964.

Shepherd's concise, accurate atlas is a classic in its field. It includes no text, no charts, no graphs—just colored maps of world history from about 2500 B.C. to 1964. Arranged chronologically, it emphasizes political history. It can best be utilized with Rand McNally's *Atlas of World History*, which provides explanatory text to explain the maps.

Statistical Abstract of Latin America. UCLA: Center of Latin American Studies, 1956—. Now biennial.

A brief but handy reference for statistical information on Latin American population, social organization, economic and financial characteristics, and foreign trade. Sources for each table and a bibliography provide help for the student seeking greater depth.

Statistical Abstract of the United States. U.S. Bureau of the Census. Washington, D.C.: Government Printing Office, 1879.— Annual.

A recognized, reliable summary of statistics on the social, political, and economic organization of the United States. It also serves as a guide to other statistical publications and sources through the introductory text to each section, the source notes for each table, and the bibliography of sources. Here one can find information of primarily national concern.

Also included are many tables for regions and individual states and statistics for the Commonwealth of Puerto Rico and other outlying areas of the United States.

Additional information for cities, counties, metropolitan areas, and other small units is available in supplements to the abstract, such as *County and City Data Book* and *Congressional District Data Book.* The *Statistical Abstract* is the most reliable source for such data as births, deaths, marriages and divorces, law enforcement, immigration, climate, recreation, elections, incomes, and many other subjects. There are a total of thirty-three subdivisions.

Statistical Yearbook. Paris: UNESCO, 1949–.

The best source for world statistics on population, education, science and technology, libraries, books, periodicals, film, radio, television, and general culture. Treating over 200 countries and territories, it frequently includes statistics from 1950, 1955, 1960, and 1965 to permit easy comparisons and trend-spotting. The material is submitted by participating nations for inclusion. The volume includes a selected list of other UNESCO statistical publications.

Part III

The Historian and His Milieu

History Departments: A Ranking

The student who is considering graduate school in history may be guided by the following list from a survey published in Kenneth D. Roose and Charles J. Andersen's *A Rating of Graduate Programs* by the American Council on Education. The earlier dates allow one to draw conclusions about the trend at a given school.

1957	1964	1969	Institution
1	1	1*	Harvard
3	3	1*	Yale
4	2	3	California, Berkeley
6	6	4	Princeton
2	4*	5*	Columbia
15	7*	5*	Stanford
5	4*	5*	Wisconsin
7	7*	8*	Chicago
12	9*	8*	Michigan
8	9*	10	Cornell
9	11	11	Johns Hopkins
#	12	12	UCLA
#	16*	13*	Indiana
11	13*	13*	Northwestern
10	13*	13*	Pennsylvania

#not ranked that year

*tied for that position

1957	*1964*	*1969*	*Institution*
#	19	16	North Carolina
#	#	17*	Brandeis
#	#	17*	Brown
#	16*	17*	Duke
13	13*	17*	Illinois
#	20	17*	Washington (Seattle)
14	16*	22	Minnesota
#	#	23*	Texas
#	#	23*	Virginia
#	#	25	Rochester

The following institutions were ranked slightly below the top twenty-five.

Bryn Mawr	Kansas	Rice
Claremont	Michigan State	Rutgers
Emory	NYU	Vanderbilt
Iowa (Iowa City)	Ohio State	Washington (St. Louis)

The following were also rated better than adequate.

Boston U.	Louisiana State	Oregon
Buffalo	Maryland	Penn State
California, Riverside	Massachusetts	Pittsburgh
Case Western Reserve	Missouri	Southern California
Colorado	Nebraska	Syracuse
Florida	Notre Dame	Tulane
Kentucky	Oklahoma	Wayne State

....

#not ranked that year

*tied for that position

Ranking The Presidents

Judging the Presidents on such criteria as defense of the national interest, defense of the public welfare, caliber of appointments, innovation, and impact, historians rank them roughly as follows:

Great

1. Abraham Lincoln
2. George Washington
3. Franklin D. Roosevelt
4. Woodrow Wilson
5. Thomas Jefferson

Near Great

6. Andrew Jackson
7. Theodore Roosevelt
8. James K. Polk
9. Harry S Truman
10. John Adams
11. Grover Cleveland

Average

12. James Madison

13. John Quincy Adams
14. Rutherford B. Hayes
15. William McKinley
16. William Howard Taft
17. Martin Van Buren
18. James Monroe
19. Herbert Hoover
20. Benjamin Harrison
21. Chester A. Arthur
22. Dwight D. Eisenhower
23. Andrew Johnson

Below Average

24. Zachary Taylor
25. John Tyler
26. Millard Fillmore

Below Average (cont.)
27. Calvin Coolidge
28. Franklin Pierce
29. James Buchanan

Failures

30. Ulysses S. Grant
31. Warren G. Harding

Unranked (too short tenure)

William Henry Harrison
James A. Garfield

Unranked (too recent for
    perspective)

John F. Kennedy
Lyndon B. Johnson
Richard M. Nixon

Leading Historical Journals

African Historical Studies (founded 1968). Semiannual.

Contains three or four long articles and several first-rate book reviews. It treats all aspects of African history, and is designed primarily for the specialist.

American Heritage (1954). Six/year.

Presents scholarly material at the popular level. It deals extensively in social, cultural, and educational aspects of American history, and occasionally devotes an entire issue to a single subject. A hardcover periodical, it is profusely illustrated and attractively presented.

American Historical Review (1895). Five/year.

The official journal of the American Historical Association, the *AHR* usually includes five lengthy articles representing original research and 150 to 200 scholarly reviews. Presupposing some basic knowledge of historiography on the part of the reader, it is one of the basic journals in college libraries and deals with all aspects of world history.

American History Illustrated. (1966). Ten/year.

Similar to *American Heritage*, this soft-cover publication makes excellent use of photographs and illustrations. Contributions are popularly written by historians or participants in the events described.

American West (1964). Quarterly.

The official publication of the Western History Association is written for both the general reader and scholar. Each issue includes eight or nine well-illustrated articles on a wide variety of topics pertaining to the western United States.

Americas (1944). Quarterly.

This popularly written, heavily illustrated review of inter-American cultural history deals with Latin America since the early sixteenth century. It has only limited circulation, but offers good objective articles.

Business History Review (1926). Quarterly.

Features scholarly articles of interest to students of both history and business. The critical book reviews are contributed by experts in both fields.

Canadian Historical Review (1920). Quarterly.

The finest Canadian history publication, *CHR's* three or four scholarly articles stress Canadian political history and foreign relations. It includes both lengthy, analytical book reviews and a list of recent publications relating to Canada.

Canadian Journal of History (1966). Three/year.

Deals primarily with world history rather than Canadian. It includes four or five well-documented articles and twenty-five to thirty critical reviews of recent historical works. Occasional articles are written in French.

Capitol Studies (1972). Two/year.

Published by the United States Capitol Historical Society, this journal includes articles on art, architecture, history, and political science as they relate to Congress and the Capitol. Sometimes a theme like lobbying provides a focal point for an issue, which includes several book reviews as well as numerous articles.

China Quarterly. (1960).

Each issue features seven to eight articles on both current and historical material in international relations, political science, economics, and law. It includes several long essay reviews and book notes. It is a "must" for China watchers.

Civil War History (1955). Quarterly.

Includes four or five articles in each issue along with lengthy critical book reviews. It treats material which in any way involves the Civil War and Reconstruction.

Current History (1922). Monthly.

This magazine of world affairs offers a fine review of history and international events for the nonspecialist. It is written in popular style by noted historians and scholars. Each issue usually devotes its six to ten articles to a specific area or topic, and includes book reviews and a news section entitled "The Month in Review."

East European Quarterly (1967).

Focuses on the history, politics, economics, and personalities of the region and includes critical reviews of books in Europe and America.

Economic History Review (1927). Three/year.

Published by England's Economic History Society, this journal deals with all aspects of economic history, though it stresses Great Britain. Several scholarly articles and forty to fifty critical book reviews are standard.

English Historical Review (1886). Quarterly.

One of the world's finest historical journals, *EHR* treats the history of all periods with an emphasis on Britain and the Empire. Four or five scholarly articles and some of the best book reviews in the field of history make this a valuable source.

Foreign Affairs (1922). Quarterly.

A prestige journal offering contributions by leading scholars, journalists, and public figures, *Foreign Affairs* deals with social, political, and economic issues of interest to the layman and the specialist. The magazine seeks to guide public opinion on current public issues by presenting divergent ideas.

Hispanic American Historical Review (1918). Quarterly.

Far more valuable than the popular *Americas,* this scholarly journal includes four or five articles, several critical book reviews, and emphasizes politics and government from the seventeenth to nineteenth centuries.

Historian (1938). Quarterly.

This journal, published by the Phi Alpha Theta National Honor Society in History, is one of the best scholarly, general historical publications available. The quality of writing is good and it contains many critical book reviews.

Historical Studies (1940). Semiannual.

This Australian publication features articles on the political, economic, and social history of Australia, New Zealand, and the Pacific from early discovery to the present.

History (1912). Three/year.

An English periodical focusing on European history, *History* generally includes five or six scholarly articles and an extensive book review section which takes up half of each issue. It is the official journal of the Historical Association.

History and Theory (1960). Three/year.

Three to five scholarly monographs and six to nine book-review essays deal primarily with the philosophy of history and historiography.

History Studies (1968). Three/year.

This scholarly English journal offers five to eight well-documented articles on English and European history of all periods.

History Today (1951). Monthly.

An illustrated historical magazine for the general reader, *History Today* treats all periods and places, although it stresses England. Six or seven popularly written articles by professional historians, fine book reviews, and helpful notes for further reading make it a very useful publication.

Horizon (1958). Quarterly.

The world history equivalent of *American Heritage,* with hard covers and glossy format. Popularly written by experts, it deals with topics ranging from archaeology to literature.

Journal of African History (1960). Three/year.

Includes numerous scholarly articles covering all stages of African history, a few illustrations, and an occasional article in French.

Journal of American History (formerly *Mississippi Valley Historical Review*) (1914). Quarterly.

This is the journal of the Organization of American Historians and ranks on a par with the *American Historical Review.* It deals exclusively with American history through scholarly articles and a large number of long, critical book reviews.

Journal of Contemporary History (1966). Quarterly.

This British journal normally focuses twelve to fifteen scholarly articles on one broad topic in twentieth-century European history. No reviews are included.

Journal of Economic History (1941). Quarterly.

This is the American equivalent to the *Economic History Review*, although it is international in scope. It features scholarly articles and critical book reviews.

Journal of Modern History (1929). Quarterly.

This honored American periodical emphasizes European history since the Renaissance. It has outstanding contributors, thoroughly documented articles, and excellent book reviews.

Journal of Negro History (1916). Quarterly.

Published by the Association for the Study of Negro Life and History, this is the most authoritative journal treating the history of the Afro-American in the United States. Three to six long articles and several excellent book reviews highlight each issue.

Journal of Social History (1967). Quarterly.

Scholarly interdisciplinary articles treat trends in social history. Each issue includes several good book reviews.

Journal of Southeast Asian History (1966). Semiannual.

Publishing scholarly articles on twentieth-century history and the other social sciences, this journal draws on many Asian contributors. It is published in English by the University of Singapore.

Journal of Southern History (1935). Quarterly.

One of the finest regional journals, the *JSH* usually has three or four scholarly articles treating the history of the southern United States. Its lengthy and critical book reviews are excellent.

Journal of the History of Ideas (1940). Quarterly.

Devoted to cultural and intellectual history, this publication generally includes eight to ten articles. Among the subjects treated are the history of philosophy, of literature and the arts, of the natural and social sciences, and of religious, political, and social movements. Occasional review articles are critical.

Labor History (1960). Three/year.

Emphasizing international labor studies and social history, this well-written journal includes an average of six articles per issue and is invaluable to those interested in the history and development of the labor movement.

Middle East Journal (1946). Quarterly.

This admirably objective periodical is designed to develop among the American people an interest in the Middle East and an appreciation of its history, culture, and political and economic affairs. It includes brief articles on all facets of the region and numerous book reviews.

Military Affairs (1937). Quarterly.

The best scholarly journal of military history. It includes detailed articles by both professional historians and members of the armed forces. Most material is well documented and emphasizes American military affairs.

New England Quarterly (1928).

Another excellent regional journal, *New England Quarterly* treats the history and culture of that section of the nation. It normally consists of four or five scholarly articles and many broad, critical book reviews.

Pacific Historical Review (1932). Quarterly.

Treats, in a scholarly way, affairs of the American West and countries bordering on the Pacific Ocean. It includes a large number of critical book reviews, and is valuable for students of the Far East.

Past and Present (1952). Three/year.

An English historical magazine, *Past and Present* is more scholarly than *History Today*. It deals with all countries and times, stressing social and economic history. It features a unique section devoted to a current debate between historians and four to seven articles of interest to the general reader.

Prologue: The Journal of the National Archives. (1969). Quarterly.

Prologue publishes scholarly articles based on the records of the federal government. It includes illustrations, documents, book notes, and information about National Archives and Record Service conferences, publications, and accessions.

Round Table (1910). Quarterly.

This London publication treats economic, racial, social, political, and educational Commonwealth problems in brief articles.

Science and Society (1936). Quarterly.

An independent Marxist journal, *Science and Society* includes about four extensive articles and several long, critical book reviews dealing with Marxist interests throughout the world.

Slavic Review: American Quarterly of Soviet and East European Studies (1941).

This readable journal includes about six major articles and a large review section. It deals with a great diversity of topics pertaining to the region. It is a basic source for Soviet and East European scholars.

Survey: A Journal of Soviet and East European Studies (1956). Quarterly.

One of the first-rate publications in the field. Experts contribute from ten to fifteen long articles on history, politics, economics, and sociology to each issue. On occasion, entire issues are devoted to a single topic, such as the fiftieth anniversary of the Russian Revolution.

William and Mary Quarterly (1892).

This highly regarded scholarly journal deals with American history and culture prior to 1815. It includes several articles and broad, critical book reviews.

Leading United States Historians

The persons selected for the lists of leading United States and world historians have been chosen on the basis of several criteria: the likelihood that undergraduates will come in contact with them in their research, their influence on historiography, their fame or notoriety, or their general expertise in a specific field. Some are journalists, some are long dead, some are renowned older historians, and some are emerging as the leaders in historical writing of the near future. Inevitably, some worthy choices have been omitted and some less worthy included; the author's judgment is responsible. An asterisk (*) following a title indicates its availability in paperback.

Henry Adams (1838-1918)

Great grandson of John Adams, Henry Adams was revolted by the political knavery of his day and withdrew, disillusioned, from active life. He wrote the masterful *History of the United States During the Administrations of Jefferson and Madison** (9 vols., 1885-1891) as his major contribution to the store of historical knowledge. He is more famous for his disillusioned autobiography, *The Education of Henry Adams** (1918), which was very much in vogue after World War I.

James Truslow Adams (1878-1949)

Unrelated to *the* Adams family, this Adams nevertheless became an authority on them and wrote a book on the family in 1930. His trilogy on New England, *The Founding of New England** (1921), *Revolutionary New England, 1691-1776* (1923), and

New England in the Republic, 1776-1850 (1926), won him renown and a Pulitzer Prize during the 1920's. A prolific as well as gifted writer, he wrote many other books, of which *The Epic of America* (1931) was most popular. He later edited the *Dictionary of American History* (1940).

Frederick Lewis Allen (1890-1954)

Either a historical journalist or a contemporary social historian, Allen had a gift for writing fascinating prose that brought alive the spirit of the times. *Only Yesterday** (1931), a history of the twenties, is the source of many of the stories and myths of the period and is still widely read. *Since Yesterday** (1940) continued the story through the thirties, and *The Big Change** (1952) outlined the broad social changes of the first half of the twentieth century. If one retains a healthy skepticism, he will find Allen a delightful guide.

Charles M. Andrews (1863-1943)

One of the giants of American colonial history, this former Yale professor wrote a brilliant essay analysis of the coming of the American Revolution in 1924. His most famous work, however, was his four-volume *The Colonial Period of American History** (1934-1938), the first volume of which won him a Pulitzer Prize. His viewpoint was imperial, his interpretation judicious, his scholarship accurate, his style vigorous, and his emphasis political and economic rather than social.

Herbert Aptheker (1915-   )

A leading theoretician of the Communist party in the United States, Aptheker is most interested in American Negro history and contemporary American thought. *American Negro Slave Revolts** (1943) is probably his most famous book, though it treads much the same ground as Garrison did a century before. His fascinating account of *Nat Turner's Slave Rebellion** (1966) shows a sympathy for violence if no other means will work. His work is well documented.

Thomas A. Bailey (1902-   )

A specialist in diplomatic history, Bailey has taught at Stanford since 1930. His *Diplomatic History of the American People* (8th ed., 1969) is a highly entertaining and enormously popular text. His *American Pageant** (4th ed., 1971) possesses the same happy quality of readability and is also widely used in colleges. He has written numerous other volumes, including *The Art of Diplomacy** (1968), in which he argues for national self-interest as the only sensible basis for foreign policy, and two books on the Paris Peace Conference and its aftermath written in 1944-45.

Bernard Bailyn (1922-   )

A colonial and revolutionary historian at Harvard, Bailyn has authored *The New England Merchants in the Seventeenth Century** (1955), suggesting that it was the merchants rather than the Puritan clergy who were the prime movers in the gradual changing of society. His *Ideological Origins of the American Revolution** (1967) is a very sensitive and significant analysis of the current viewpoint on the coming of the Revolution.

George Bancroft (1800-1891)

Known as "the father of American history," Bancroft wrote a ten-volume *History of the United States** (1834-74), the first complete work on the subject. His assembly and utilization of original material contributed to later "scientific history." A Jacksonian Democrat and occasional civil servant, he sympathized in his work with the twin themes of nationalism and democracy, exhibited faith in progress and the essential worth of mankind, and employed a style tinged with the enthusiasm of an old-style patriotic orator.

Charles Beard (1874-1948)

One of the most influential historians of the twentieth century, Beard is most noted for his economic interpretation of history. *An Economic Interpretation of the Constitution** (1913) challenged the deity of the founding fathers and suggested that their motivation was their own economic self-interest rather than primarily the nation's welfare. This view was part of a progressive framework which saw American history in terms of a struggle of the people against the special interests. Rather than idealizing the past as a golden age, the Progressives believed the twentieth century would see the triumph of the "people." In his last years Beard became disenchanted with Roosevelt and in *President Roosevelt and the Coming of the War, 1941* (1948) blamed the President for leading the United States into World War II deliberately. He wrote a large number of other books, some in collaboration with his wife Mary; his importance is profound.

Carl Becker (1873-1945)

A longtime Cornell professor and author of the brilliant *The Declaration of Independence** (1922), Becker is perhaps best remembered for his American Historical Association presidential address of 1931, "Everyman His Own Historian." In it he defined history as "the memory of things said and done," as opposed to what actually happened, a defense of the personal involvement of Progressive historians in their work, or historical relativism.

George Beer (1872-1920)

Author of several books on the British colonial system, Beer was a member of the Imperial school of history. He attempted to view the American Revolution from London's viewpoint rather than Boston's and thus added considerable balance to the earlier nationalist interpretation which made little effort to understand both sides of the dispute.

Samuel Flagg Bemis (1891-   )

One of the giants of this century, Bemis was long a professor at Yale. He was twice the recipient of Pulitzer Prizes, first for his account of *Pinckney's Treaty* (1926) and later for the first volume of his superb two-volume biography of John Quincy Adams. *John Quincy Adams and the Foundation of American Foreign Policy** (1949) and *John Quincy Adams and the Union* (1956) combine to form perhaps the best biography of any

American. He specializes in diplomatic history and has authored a text on that topic and also co-authored *A Guide to the Diplomatic History of the United States* (1935), the basic source book for the field. His work was often rather technical for the casual reader, but he earned a reputation as a historian's historian.

Barton J. Bernstein (1936-   )

This Stanford professor is a revisionist specializing in twentieth-century American history and particularly the Cold War. He has edited a volume of documents critical of the Truman administration (1966), but his most important work was editing *Towards a New Past: Dissenting Essays in American History** (1968). This chronological sequence of articles offers a New Left interpretation of the full sweep of American history; some of the articles are excellent, some provocative, some of questionable scholarship, but the collection provides the basic introduction to the New Left view of history.

Ray Billington (1903-   )

A specialist in frontier history, Billington wrote *Westward Expansion* (1940). Although fairly difficult to read, it is the best treatment of the subject and includes an outstanding seventy-five page bibliographical essay. A disciple of Frederick Jackson Turner, this former president of the Organization of American Historians (1962-63) is presently Senior Research Associate at the Huntington Library in Los Angeles.

John Blum (1921-   )

This Yale professor specializes in recent American history. Two of his most popular books are the brief *The Republican Roosevelt** (1954), a brilliant, thoughtful, well-written sketch of TR, and *Woodrow Wilson and the Politics of Morality** (1957), another well-conceived and well-written volume. They were among the first critical assessments of these two Presidents. He has also edited *From the Morgenthau Diaries* (3 vols., 1959-67) on the New Deal period.

Daniel Boorstin (1914-   )

A longtime University of Chicago professor, Boorstin has an original mind full of ideas on American social and intellectual history. *The Genius of American Politics** (1953) is a classic concensus interpretation of American history suggesting that our traditions and political framework are all basically conservative. His fascinating, award-winning *The Americans: The Colonial Experience** (1958) and *The Americans: The National Experience** (1965) are veritable treasure-troves of trivia that afford scholar and layman alike intriguing new insights into the nation's past. *The Americans: The Democratic Experience* (1973) concludes his distinctive three-volume survey of American history.

Claude Bowers (1879-1958)

A journalist and diplomat, Bowers wrote a trilogy on Thomas Jefferson: *Young Jefferson** (1945), *Jefferson and Hamilton** (1925), and *Jefferson in Power** (1936). Though easy reading, they constitute a brilliant piece of special pleading; Bowers idolized Jefferson, and the books must be read with that point firmly in mind. He also wrote a well-documented volume on Reconstruction, *The Tragic Era** (1929).

Irving Brant (1885-   )

Brant wrote the definitive biography of *James Madison* (6 vols., 1941-61) in an effort to lift Madison to the first rank among the Presidents. That he failed was the fault of Madison, not Brant; the book is at times too laudatory and, as is almost inevitable with such a work, a bit too detailed in places. Brant has condensed the six volumes into *The Fourth President: A Life of James Madison* (1970), which is not as high in quality as the original.

Carl Bridenbaugh (1903-   )

President of the American Historical Association in 1962 and professor at Brown University, Bridenbaugh wrote two widely acclaimed volumes on urban life in colonial America: *Cities in the Wilderness, 1625-1742** (1939) and *Cities in Revolt: Urban*

Life in America, 1743-1776* (1955). Original, highly readable treatments of Boston, New York, Newport, Philadelphia, and Charles Town, they are indispensable sources for pre-revolution study. In *Myths and Realities** (1963) he offered some significant new views of the colonial South.

James MacGregor Burns (1918-   )

A professor of political science at Williams College, Burns has written the best completed biography of Franklin Roosevelt, a two-volume political study. *Roosevelt: The Lion and the Fox** (1956) takes a balanced approach, pointing out both strengths and weaknesses in a calm, scholarly way. *Roosevelt: The Soldier of Freedom* (1970) is a fairly critical assessment of FDR's wartime leadership. Until Frank Freidel or Arthur Schlesinger finish their multi-volume treatments, this is likely to be the standard work.

W. J. Cash (1900-1941)

The Mind of the South* (1941) was Cash's sole contribution to history, but it is a minor classic critically analyzing the social background, temperament, and characteristic ways of the Southerner. A knowledgeable interpretive work, it relates the ante-bellum period to the "New South" and that to the twentieth-century society of the region in a persuasive, penetrating treatment.

Bruce Catton (1899-   )

Writing full-time about the Civil War since 1952, Catton has compiled a long list of titles, including a trilogy on the Army of the Potomac, a brilliant one-volume history of the military course of the war (*This Hallowed Ground*)*, and *American Heritage's History of the Civil War*. He combines historical accuracy with poetic insight, and his descriptive abilities are such that the books appear to be written in full color. For clarity, objectivity, expertise, color, and volume, Catton cannot be improved upon.

Thomas Cochran (1902-   )

A professor at the University of Pennsylvania, Cochran wrote *The Age of Enterprise** (1942) with William Miller. It is a lively, readable account of industrial America from 1800 to 1930. The title essay from *The Inner Revolution* (1965) offers brilliant insights into the growth of relativism in American life and is a basic source for social-intellectual history. Cochran's area of specialization, however, is economic history.

Henry Steele Commager (1902-   )

One of the prominent names in American intellectual history, Commager was an outspoken defender of freedom of thought during the McCarthy era, suggesting that the greatest danger facing America was an absence of thought. He authored *The American Mind** (1951), a critical patriotic history, and numerous other volumes. He is perhaps best known for *The Growth of the American Republic* (1931), a classic American history text he co-authored with Samuel Eliot Morison which is now a bit dated on minority history. In addition, his *Documents in American History* (1934) is still the finest one-volume collection of primary materials.

Avery Craven (1886-   )

This distinguished Civil War historian has served as president of both the American Historical Association (1930) and the Organization of American Historians (1962). In a controversial work, he blamed *The Coming of the Civil War** (1942) on immoderate leaders of the era. *The Growth of Southern Nationalism, 1848-61* (1953) is clearly one of the finest treatments of the period by perhaps the most knowledgeable man on the immediate prewar era.

Richard Current (1912-   )

A professor at the University of North Carolina, Current is particularly interested in the Civil War and Reconstruction period and in diplomatic history. His thorough *Old Thad Stevens* (1942) and the speculative and fascinating *The Lincoln Nobody Knows** (1958) deal with the trials of disunion; his

Secretary Stimson (1954) is a critical assessment of Franklin Roosevelt's Secretary of War.

Merle Curti (1897-   )

Long a professor at the University of Wisconsin and elected president of both the American Historical Association (1953) and the Organization of American Historians (1950), Curti's major contribution to historical literature is *The Growth of American Thought* (1943). This Pulitzer Prize-winning synthesis of American intellectual history, with its excellent bibliography, is very useful for the studious reader. Drawing on a vast amount of research, Curti has written a cool and dispassionate account.

Alexander DeConde (1920-   )

Since 1961 the diplomatic historian at the University of California, Santa Barbara, DeConde has written a number of important books in his field. *Herbert Hoover's Latin-American Policy* (1951) is a straightforward and readable, if too brief, account which was part of a general reassessment of Hoover in the early 1950s. *The American Secretary of State: An Interpretation* (1962) is a crisply written collection of judgments and analyses which concludes with a list of the ten greatest secretaries by DeConde's criteria. In 1972 he authored *Half-Bitter, Half-Sweet,* an impressive and elegant treatment of Italian-American relations since the 1600s that should command a wide audience. In addition, DeConde has written a fine textbook, *A History of American Foreign Policy** (1963).

Carl Degler (1921-   )

This Stanford professor has written several books, but his most important is *Out of Our Past: The Forces that Shaped Modern America** (1959). A lively, illuminating, interpretive work, it seeks to answer the question, "How did we get the way we are today?" It employs a rather scattershot approach and has been criticized for what it omits, but the perceptive idealism of what is included makes it a valuable book. *Neither Black Nor White** (1971), appraising the Brazilian situation, is an important recent contribution to the comparative approach to slavery.

Bernard DeVoto (1897-1955)

A novelist and critic, DeVoto found that his writing ability served history well. Very interested in the West, he wrote *The Year of Decision, 1846** (1943), *Across the Wide Missouri** (1947), and *The Course of Empire** (1952), a superbly written history of the region.

Robert A. Divine (1929-   )

A diplomatic historian at the University of Texas, Divine has written three fine volumes on American foreign policy between 1930 and 1945: *The Illusion of Neutrality** (1962), *The Reluctant Belligerent** (1965), and *The Second Chance* (1967). His books are both well written and scholarly.

David Donald (1920-   )

One of the nation's foremost experts on the Civil War period, Donald is a professor at Johns Hopkins University. He has written the fascinating collection of reappraisals of Lincoln entitled *Lincoln Reconsidered** (1961), *The Politics of Reconstruction, 1863-1867** (1965), and his excellent *Charles Sumner and the Coming of the Civil War* (1960), the first part of a biography of one of the most controversial figures in American history. Donald is perceptive, original, and literate—a fine historian.

W. E. B. DuBois (1868-1963)

DuBois was the champion of complete Negro equality, a position generally contrasted with Booker T. Washington's conciliatory policy. Very active in the NAACP, he nevertheless found time to write several books. *The Souls of Black Folk** (1903) was surpassed by *Black Reconstruction** (1935), a bitter, Marxist attack on injustice and racial inequality. Far from impartial, it received mixed reviews, partly because the time had not yet arrived when the Negro could speak out and be heard, and partly because of the author's bias. It is nevertheless an important revisionist work and foreshadowed many other books in the 1950s and 1960s.

William A. Dunning (1857-1922)

Dunning's influence on American historiography has been great. As a professor at Columbia he shaped many of the Progressive historians' attitudes on Reconstruction in the direction suggested by his *Reconstruction: Political and Economic* * (1907). The attitude, dominant through World War II, was that Reconstruction had been a terrible mistake, that the Negro had in fact been inferior, and that the North had been shameful in trying to force the blacks on the whites as equals. This was the sort of attitude that made DuBois bitter.

Stanley Elkins (1927-   )

This Smith College professor has written one of the most important books of recent decades: *Slavery: A Problem in American Institutional and Intellectual Life* * (1959). It set off a huge debate over slavery by seeking to understand the whys rather than the whats of the institution. Elkins provoked considerable criticism for comparing slaves with Jews in concentration camps, and much discussion of his contrasting slavery in Cuba with that in Virginia. The response has been such that Ann Lane has edited *The Debate Over "Slavery"* * (1971) which brings together many of the reactions.

Harold U. Faulkner (1890-1968)

Faulkner is most noted for *The Decline of Laissez-faire, 1897-1917* (1951), a brilliant, discerning interpretation of the factors involved in the growth of big business and government regulation.

Herbert Feis (1893-1972)

Working in the State Department on the eve of World War II, Feis gained firsthand experience which helped him write *Road to Pearl Harbor* * (1950), a well-documented, balanced, sometimes dry account of the years 1937 to 1941. His best works were a two-volume sequence dealing with wartime diplomacy: *Churchill-Roosevelt-Stalin* * (1957) and *Between War and Peace: The Potsdam Conference* * (1960). The latter won a Pulitzer

Prize. Admirably fair if not always first rate in style, these two volumes are essential works for the student of World War II diplomacy.

Sidney Fine (1920-   )

A specialist on labor and economic history at the University of Michigan, Fine has authored the distinguished *Laissez-faire and the General Welfare State: A Study of Conflict in American Thought, 1865-1901** (1956). The book treats all sides of the issue with objectivity and shows great research, though it offers little material of significant originality.

John Hope Franklin (1915-   )

A Negro professor at the University of Chicago, Franklin has written *From Slavery to Freedom** (1967), probably still the best history of the American Negro despite stylistic limitations. His best book is *Reconstruction After the Civil War** (1961), a dispassionate, balanced, and well-written interpretation based on careful research. Concentrating primarily upon political matters, he suggests that radical rule was moderate rather than excessive, and that corruption was rampant throughout the country, not just in the South.

Douglas S. Freeman (1886-1953)

Long the editor of the *Richmond News-Leader,* Freeman often rose at 2:00 A.M. to write his history, and he produced three outstanding achievements. *R. E. Lee* (4 vols., 1934) won a Pulitzer Prize and is the definitive biography of the general. *Lee's Lieutenants* (3 vols., 1942-44) is excellent military history and entertaining reading. *George Washington: A Biography* (7 vols., 1948-57), a monumental achievement and another definitive biography of a great Virginian, rested on massive research and full-time work until Freeman's death.

Frank Freidel (1916-   )

The author of several short books on FDR, this Harvard professor stopped halfway through his masterwork, a proposed seven-volume biography of Roosevelt. The three volumes completed

(*The Apprenticeship, The Ordeal,* and *The Triumph*) were all completed by 1956 and carry FDR's career down only to the governorship of New York. It is indeed unfortunate that the author appears to have abandoned this distinguished work.

John A. Garraty (1920-   )

A Columbia professor, Garraty has written brief biographies of *Henry Cabot Lodge* (1953) and *Woodrow Wilson** (1956) as well as a popular text, *The American Nation. The New Commonwealth** (1968) treats the 1877-90 period as a watershed when people began dealing with their problems collectively rather than as individuals and laissez-faire proved no longer viable. The notes are extensive and the bibliography is good, but the book has no deep analysis.

Paul W. Gates (1901-   )

A longtime Cornell specialist in American agricultural history, Gates wrote a number of books on the subject. His best was *Fifty Million Acres: Conflicts over Kansas Land Policy, 1854-1890** (1954). A brief, lucid account, it makes an important contribution to understanding agrarian unrest; his scholarship is meticulous.

Eugene Genovese (1930-   )

Genovese, professor at Sir George Williams University in Montreal, is most noted for *The Political Economy of Slavery** (1965). He relates economic questions to class structure, social institutions, ideology, and politics in the antebellum South in a highly recommended, thought-provoking, insight-filled book. His knowledge of the sources and secondary works is admirable.

Lawrence Gipson (1909-1971)

This Pulitzer Prize-winning Imperial historian, professor of history at Lehigh University for almost thirty years, wrote one of the most ambitious historical enterprises undertaken in this century. *The British Empire before the American Revolution* (14 vols., 1939-1968) is an exhaustive analysis of the coming of the revolt and concludes that once France left North America,

the Revolution was inevitable. *The Coming of the Revolution**
(1954) is a judicious, balanced synopsis of the major work in
the New American Nation series.

Eric Goldman (1915-   )

This Princeton professor has written two very popular books:
*Rendezvous with Destiny** (1952) discusses liberalism in
America since the Civil War and concludes that the 1948 election was a turning point—a liberal victory in time of peace and
prosperity. *The Crucial Decade and After** (1960) is a more
detailed look at the years since World War II. It is well written,
full of pithy quotes and commentary on the life of the American people. Goldman concluded that the Americans would
continue to reform government and pursue an internationalist
foreign policy.

Norman Graebner (1915-   )

A diplomatic historian at the University of Virginia, Graebner
has written several books of note. *Empire on the Pacific* (1955)
suggested Eastern commercial interests were more than a little
interested in acquiring Oregon and California as steps to the
Orient. *The New Isolationism* (1956) notes conservative political influence on Truman's and Eisenhower's foreign policies.
He also edited the valuable *An Uncertain Tradition: American
Secretaries of State in the Twentieth Century** (1961).

Oscar Handlin (1915-   )

A specialist in immigration history at Harvard, Handlin won a
Pulitzer Prize for *The Uprooted** (1951), a superb account of
the various obstacles an immigrant had to overcome before
getting settled in the United States. In addition, since 1951 he
has been the editor of Little, Brown's Library of American
Biography, to which he contributed *Al Smith and His America**
(1958).

John D. Hicks (1890-   )

Hicks wrote the classic *The Populist Revolt** in 1931 and was
elected president of the Mississippi Valley Historical Association

the following year. He has never matched that achievement—
The Republican Ascendancy, 1921-1933* (1960) is a disap-
pointment in the New American Nation series. *The Populist
Revolt,* however, was the first complete history of the movement and is filled with insight, information, and humor. A
scholarly work with an exhaustive bibliography, it is still the
basic source for Populism.

John Higham (1920-   )

A specialist on social, intellectual, and cultural history at the
University of Michigan, Higham has written *Strangers in the
Land** (1955), a scholarly, judicious, and astute account of the
nativist movement between 1860 and 1925. He also co-edited
Reconstruction of American History* (1962), a useful histori-
graphical study.

Richard Hofstadter (1916-1970)

The sudden death of this longtime Columbia professor in 1970
was a major blow to the historical profession—he was indeed a
giant in the field. His highly readable, stimulating books provoked controversy and widespread admiration. *The American
Political Tradition** (1948) contains a series of perceptive biographical sketches of great Americans. *Social Darwinism in
American Thought** (1955) is the standard work on the subject.
The Age of Reform* (1955), an attempt to tie together the
Populist, Progressive, and New Deal movements, offers many
fresh insights. *Anti-Intellectualism in American Life** (1963)
traces the religious and business roots of anti-intellectualism
back to the Puritans. *The Progressive Historians** (1968) is an
incisive analysis of Turner, Beard, and Parrington and his last
major work.

Matthew Josephson (1899-   )

Primarily a literary critic, Matthew Josephson contributed two
books in the thirties. *The Politicos** (1938) is a rather dull,
scholarly criticism of the late nineteenth century's politicians.
The Robber Barons* (1934) introduced a common term to the
language and represented a timely reinterpretation of the great

businessmen of the same period in light of Josephson's leftist sympathies and the general anti-business mood of the Depression.

Robert Kelley (1925-   )

Since 1955 a historian at the University of California, Santa Barbara, Kelley made a major contribution to comparative intellectual history in 1969 with *The Transatlantic Persuasion: The Liberal-Democratic Mind in the Age of Gladstone.* Successfully sketching comparisons between Tilden and Cleveland in the United States, Brown and Mackenzie in Canada, and Gladstone in England, Kelley demonstrates that there was a common persuasion guiding the liberals in all three nations.

George F. Kennan (1904-   )

Scholar, Princeton professor, and diplomat, Kennan has been a prominent figure in Russian-American relations since the War. His *American Diplomacy 1900-1950** (1951) called for a return to positive power relationships in diplomacy and an end to legalistic, moralistic approaches. *Russia and the West Under Lenin and Stalin** (1961), one of several books he wrote on Russian relations, was a call for the West to be flexible toward the Kremlin. His *Memoirs, 1925-1950** are a brilliant subjective evaluation of his years in the nation's service and a valuable book for understanding the policies of those years. A second volume (1972) carries the story down to 1963.

Edward C. Kirkland (1894-   )

A longtime economic historian at Bowdoin, Kirkland authored *Dream and Thought in the Business Community, 1860-1900** (1956), a well-researched and well-written account of what business leaders thought, or thought they thought. *Industry Comes of Age** (1967) is a massive, comprehensive account of the years 1860 to 1897 which synthesizes the changes in business, labor, and public policy. This stimulating book emphasizes the accomplishments rather than the failings of the "robber barons."

Adrienne Koch (1912-1971)

Teaching at the University of Maryland, Adrienne Koch specialized in the philosophical, moral, and political thought of enlightenment figures in the United States, especially Thomas Jefferson. Among her superbly written books, *Power, Morals, and the Founding Fathers** (1962) stands out for its expert sketches of the great leaders of the republic's early years.

Gabriel Kolko (1931-   )

A leading revisionist historian, Kolko has authored two books which challenge conventional wisdom. *The Triumph of Conservatism, 1900-1916** (1963) suggests that businessmen, far from opposing the Progressive reforms, actually led in the fight for their adoption as a means of preserving their own influence. *The Limits of Power, 1945-1954** (1972), written with his wife Joyce, is a heavily documented account of American foreign policy during those years from a perspective sympathetic to Russia. Although not entirely convincing, it is clearly the finest presentation of that viewpoint.

Christopher Lasch (1932-   )

This leftist historian has made two important contributions to the understanding of the American Left. *The New Radicalism in America, 1889-1963** (1965) is a critique of radical men and women thinkers who sought or seek to transform society. It is brilliantly thought out but difficult to read. *The Agony of the American Left** (1969) is a provocative anti-American analysis holding that the Left has been only a marginal force in American politics.

Richard W. Leopold (1912-   )

A specialist in American diplomatic history and naval affairs at Northwestern University, Leopold has written *Elihu Root and the Conservative Tradition** (1954) in the Library of American Biography. *The Growth of American Foreign Policy* (1962) is the finest text on the subject, delving deeply into the constitutional ramifications of foreign policy control while treating the material with a meticulous exactness. The dense writing makes reading difficult. In a long-needed innovation, Leopold devotes five-sixths of the book to the post-1890 period rather than seeking chronological balance.

William Leuchtenburg (1922-   )

A professor at Columbia, Leuchtenburg is a gifted writer specializing in recent American history. His *Perils of Prosperity, 1914-1932** (1958) is the most popular treatment of the period, complete with many of Frederick Lewis Allen's stories and an equally readable text. *Franklin D. Roosevelt and the New Deal, 1932-1940** (1963), one of the finest volumes in the New American Nation series, is still the best one-volume account of the thirties.

Arthur S. Link (1920-   )

Link, teaching at Wilson's old school, Princeton, has now completed five volumes of his definitive biography of that President. Thorough, objective, accurate, and interpretive, it ranks as one of the finest examples of American biography. Along the way Link has produced some briefer volumes: *Wilson the Diplomatist** (1957) and *Woodrow Wilson and the Progressive Era, 1910-1917** (1954). He is also the co-editor of the Wilson papers, of which five volumes have now appeared.

Staughton Lynd (1929-   )

This noteworthy historian is most important as a symbol of the academic wing of the New Left. He led an effort to gain the presidency of the American Historical Association in 1969 and visited Hanoi in search of peace. His most important book, more polemical than historical, is *Intellectual Origins of American Radicalism** (1968). He co-authored *The Resistance* (1971), a sympathetic appraisal of the anti-war movement of the sixties.

John B. McMasters (1852-1932)

During his long career at the University of Pennsylvania, McMasters became the first United States history professor to combine teaching with research and writing. His masterwork was *The History of the People of the United States* (8 vols., 1883-1913), which was strongly nationalistic but avoided hero worship. He was the first prominent American social and intellectual historian.

Dumas Malone (1892-   )

After serving as editor-in-chief for volumes seven through twenty of the *Dictionary of American Biography*, Malone has concentrated most of his energy on his superb biography of Thomas Jefferson. *Jefferson the Virginian** (1948), *Jefferson and the Rights of Man** (1951), *Jefferson and the Ordeal of Liberty** (1962), and *Jefferson the President: First Term, 1801-1805** (1970) carry the story down to 1805 in a work embodying American historical scholarship at its very best. The books are learned, gracious, temperate, and just.

Ernest R. May (1928-   )

Specializing in diplomatic history at Harvard, May has written several books of importance. Probably the most acclaimed is *The World War and American Isolation, 1914-1917** (1959), which utilized the primary sources of all the major nations involved and concluded that Europe unwillingly dragged the United States into a war that the Americans were reluctant to enter. The book is a model of research, analysis, and writing.

Henry F. May (1915-   )

May, a professor of intellectual history at the University of California, has written two important books. *Protestant Churches and Industrial America** (1949) is objective and inclusive, though it tends to accept, despite some evidence to the contrary, the theory that liberal theology produced liberal social views while conservative theology produced conservative social attitudes. *The End of American Innocence** (1959) is a provocative book which argues, not altogether convincingly, that the intellectual change of the twenties actually began between 1912 and 1917 rather than being caused by World War I.

Marvin Meyers (1921-   )

This Brandeis professor caused an upheaval in the study of Jacksonian America in 1957 with *The Jacksonian Persuasion.**

An imaginative, provocative book, it suggests that the "persuasion" was conservative, looking to a golden agrarian age in the past, rather than the liberal futurist attitude suggested by Arthur Schlesinger, Jr. The nostalgia interpretation is reminiscent of Hofstadter's *The Age of Reform* view of Populism which appeared just two years before Meyers received his Ph.D. from Columbia.

John C. Miller (1907-   )

This Stanford professor is probably the leading authority on the Federalist period in the United States. *The Federalist Era, 1789-1801** (1960), part of the New American Nation series, is clear, readable, and fresh, combines synthesis with original interpretation, and is the standard work on the decade. He has also authored books on Hamilton, the Alien and Sedition Acts, and the coming and fighting of the Revolution.

Perry Miller (1905-1963)

Miller brought alive seventeenth-century New England for the twentieth century, delving into the original sources with imaginative inquiry and substituting reality for the stereotypes which had so long prevailed. His two books *The New England Mind: From Colony to Province** (1939) and *The New England Mind: The Seventeenth Century** (1954) are classics. His biographies of *Roger Williams** (1953) and *Jonathan Edwards* (1949), while difficult reading because of their profundity, are superb intellectual history. *Errand Into the Wilderness** (1956) collects a number of essays, including the title article which is found in almost every anthology. He edited the writings of *The Puritans** (1938) and ranged out of the period to edit *The Transcendentalists** (1950) and write numerous other books. He was truly one of the greatest historians in the profession.

Edmund S. Morgan (1916-   )

A student of Perry Miller at Harvard, this Yale professor has succeeded his mentor as the leading historian of Puritanism. Among his many books on the subject (he has also written two on the coming of the Revolution) are *The Puritan Dilemma**

(1958), a biography of John Winthrop, and *Roger Williams: The Church and the State** (1967), a superb analysis of the man's thought. Combining a delightful writing style with top scholarship and a sympathy for the Puritan point of view, Morgan is Miller's worthy successor.

H. Wayne Morgan (1934-   )

A University of Oklahoma professor specializing in the 1877-1914 period, Morgan has written *Eugene V. Debs: Socialist for President* (1962), *William McKinley and His America* (1963), a sympathetic account, and *America's Road to Empire* (1965), a very good, concise treatment of the Spanish-American War and its origins.

Samuel Eliot Morison (1887-   )

Long a professor at Harvard, Morison has written prolifically about colonial New England and maritime history. Modeling himself on Francis Parkman, he has sought to live and feel the history he writes, and the authenticity makes his brilliant writing fascinating. He has authored two Pulitzer Prize-winning biographies: *Admiral of the Ocean Sea: A Life of Christopher Columbus* (1942) and *John Paul Jones** (1959). His *Oxford History of the American People* (1965) has been very popular. His most awe-inspiring project is the fifteen-volume *History of United States Naval Operations in World War II* (1947-62), which despite some errors appears to be the definitive work on the subject. His list of other titles seems endless.

Richard B. Morris (1904-   )

Co-editor of the New American Nation series and editor of the *Encyclopedia of American History,* this Columbia professor has a long list of additional volumes to his credit. Probably his finest writing produced *The Peacemakers* (1965), a treatment of the conclusion of the Revolutionary War. Based on monumental research and thoroughly documented, this detailed study is not for the general reader, but is vital to students of the period.

George E. Mowry (1909-   )

A former president of the Organization of American Historians (1965), Mowry now teaches at the University of North Carolina. He has written *The California Progressives** (1952), still the best treatment of the subject. His *Era of Theodore Roosevelt, 1900-1912** (1958), in the New American Nation series, is a fine contribution to the literature of the period, well researched and well documented in addition to being very readable. *The Urban Nation** (1965) traces American history from 1920 to 1960 and stresses the impact of urbanization on the American character.

Allan Nevins (1890-1971)

One of the most prolific writers among American historians, Nevins concentrated on biography before World War II and afterward specialized in the Civil War period. He authored Pulitzer Prize-winning biographies of *Grover Cleveland* (1932) and *Hamilton Fish* (1936), plus a somewhat sympathetic *Life of John D. Rockefeller* (1940). His Civil War series is collectively known as the *Ordeal of the Union* (8 vols., 1947-71) and covers the period from 1846 to 1865 in great depth. His writing is well balanced, judicious, thorough, conscientious, and fairly readable; it places him in the first rank among recent historians.

Roy F. Nichols (1896-   )

Long a professor at the University of Pennsylvania, Nichols is a specialist in the pre-Civil War decade. He wrote *The Democratic Machine, 1850-54* (1923) and a discriminating biography of *Franklin Pierce* (1931) before completing his best work, the Pulitzer Prize-winning *The Disruption of American Democracy** (1948). The latter provides an excellent analysis of the breakdown of the Democratic party during Buchanan's administration.

Herbert L. Osgood (1855-1918)

An excellent teacher at Columbia, Osgood was an American colonial historian of the Imperial school. He was perhaps the first American professor to question the legality of the Revolution. His *The American Colonies in the Seventeenth Century* (3 vols., 1904-07) and *The American Colonies in the Eighteenth Century* (4 vols., 1924) emphasized the struggles between the British executives and the colonial assemblies.

Saul K. Padover (1905-   )

A political scientist, Padover has made several noteworthy contributions to American history. His finest book is *The Genius of America** (1960), a superb collection of analytic essays on the greatest American leaders in politics, philosophy, and the arts. His style is delightful.

Francis Parkman (1823-1893)

Near the top of any list of great American historians, Parkman combined the techniques of a careful scholar with the artistic sense of a poet. In order to write his monumental history of the Anglo-French struggle for North America, Parkman went into the wilderness to get the feel of it and capture the spirit of the time. His use of original sources was close to a pioneer effort for an American historian. After writing *The California and Oregon Trail** (1849), he spent the rest of his life writing eleven volumes of colorful prose of the struggle which culminated in 1763. *The History of the Conspiracy of Pontiac** and *Montcalm and Wolfe** are two of the most famous titles.

Vernon Parrington (1871-1929)

This liberal, almost radical giant among Progressive historians, a teacher at the University of Washington, is primarily remembered for *Main Currents in American Thought** (3 vols., 1927-30). He received a Pulitzer Prize for the second volume and died before completing the third, but the achievement was already great. Primarily a history of American literature (Parrington was an English professor), the work is a vibrant defense of American democracy which at times appears less than judicious and open to challenge for its bias. It shaped the opinions of a generation with its negative portrait of the Puritans as being outside the rational, humanist, democratic American mainstream.

Bradford Perkins (1925-   )

A University of Michigan professor specializing in Anglo-American relations, Perkins has written a trilogy on the 1795-1823 period. The volumes are filled with insight and understanding, are written dynamically and with humor, and represent the finished product of scholarly research by a literary craftsman. *The Great Rapprochement: England and the United States, 1895-1914* (1968) is a valuable study of those relations which is both witty and profound. Perkins well deserves his outstanding reputation as a scholar.

Dexter Perkins (1889-   )

A former president of the American Historical Association (1956), Perkins specializes in the Monroe Doctrine. *Hands Off: A History of the Monroe Doctrine** (1941) is a widely acclaimed scholarly treatment of the subject which is brief, clear, and written in an entertaining style which appeals to the general reader.

Stow Persons (1913-   )

- Professor at the University of Iowa, Persons is the author of *American Minds* (1958), a book seeking to describe the five principal focal concentrations of ideas, or "minds," that have formed the outline of American intellectual life during its historical development. It provides an excellent introduction to American intellectual history, although there is a gap between 1660 and 1740.

Merrill D. Peterson (1921-   )

This University of Virginia professor has edited one and written two books about Jefferson. *The Jefferson Image in the American Mind** (1960) is a fascinating account of the course of Jefferson's reputation since his death which explains why he has not always been as highly regarded as he is today. It is must reading for students of the third President.

Ulrich B. Phillips (1877-1934)

Phillips, who spent most of his teaching career at the University of Michigan, was the leading defender of the Old South. A

major figure in the historiography of the South, he wrote
*American Negro Slavery** (1919) and *Life and Labor in the Old
South** (1929), which were the standard works until some time
after World War II. His books are very readable, but his assump-
tions of inequality are now considerably out-of-date.

David M. Potter (1910-1971)
Though he has written mainly on the Civil War period (*Lincoln
and His Party in the Secession Crisis** and *The South and the
Sectional Crisis*), this Stanford professor made his major contribution with *People of Plenty** (1954). This foray into sociological history argues that abundance has been the determining
factor in forming the American character, not democracy.
Potter notes that, in our efforts to remake the world in our own
image, we are unfortunately far more able and willing to export
democracy than the abundance necessary to make it work.

Henry Pringle (1897-1958)
This journalist wrote two outstanding biographies of American
presidents: *Theodore Roosevelt: A Biography** (1931), which
won a Pulitzer Prize, and *The Life and Times of William
Howard Taft* (2 vols., 1939). The latter, based on Taft's papers
and somewhat sympathetic toward its subject, is an admirable
example of a fine scholarly portrait.

Benjamin Quarles (1904-   )
Quarles is a specialist in Negro history at Morgan State College.
He has written a solid account of *The Negro in the Civil War**
(1953), the objective, very readable *The Negro in the American
Revolution** (1961), and *The Negro in the Making of America**
(1964). His books are all characterized by exhaustive research.

James G. Randall (1881-1953)
This highly regarded Civil War historian served as president of
the American Historical Association (1952) and the Mississippi
Valley Historical Association (1939-40). Though he authored
many books on Lincoln and the Civil War, his ambition was to
write a biography of that President, undertaken without hero
worship and utilizing all available primary sources. He achieved

his goal in *Lincoln the President** (4 vols., 1945-55), with Richard Current completing the final volume after Randall's death. It is the finest biography of Lincoln and punctures many old myths such as the Ann Rutledge romance.

James Ford Rhodes (1848-1927)

Rhodes won immediate and almost unanimous acclaim for his *History of the United States from the Compromise of 1850* [to 1877]* (7 vols., 1893-1906). His fair-minded approach, thoroughness, and skill in handling vast materials make this a landmark in American historiography despite his rather pedestrian style.

Clinton Rossiter (1917-   )

A conservative political science professor at Cornell, Rossiter has contributed some noteworthy volumes to American history. *Seedtime of the Republic** (1953) is perhaps the finest book on the political ideas of the colonies prior to 1776. *Alexander Hamilton and the Constitution** (1964), in a sense a continuation of *Seedtime,* seeks to restore Hamilton to the limelight he had long lost to Jefferson. The provocative book reflects Rossiter's political views. He makes a case for 1787 as the most fateful year in American history in *1787: The Grand Convention** (1966), though perhaps a bit more truculently than necessary.

Carl Sandburg (1878-1967)

Though primarily a poet, this Socialist is important to the history student for his biography of Lincoln. *Abraham Lincoln: The Prairie Years* (2 vols., 1926) and *Abraham Lincoln: The War Years* (4 vols., 1940) constitute one of the greatest American biographies. The latter part won a Pulitzer Prize in history, though there was some criticism of Sandburg for being a bit too creative rather than completely objective. His object was to counteract earlier sentimental biographies, and he largely succeeded. The six volumes were condensed into *Abraham Lincoln: The Prairie Years and the War Years,** a one-volume abridgment, in 1954.

Arthur M. Schlesinger, Sr. (1888-1965)

For thirty years a professor at Harvard and in 1942 the president of the American Historical Association, Schlesinger wrote a large number of books on all aspects of American history, though he concentrated on the colonial period. *The Colonial Merchants and the American Revolution** (1918), a well-written account, *The Rise of the City** (1933), an engrossing, informative volume, *Paths to the Present** (1949), a collection of articles, and *Prelude to Independence: The Newspaper War on Britain, 1764-76* (1957) are just a few of his many titles.

Arthur M. Schlesinger, Jr. (1917-   )

A liberal historian at City University of New York after his service under Kennedy, Schlesinger has written two important biographies: *The Age of Jackson** (1945), which has shaped the basic attitudes toward Jackson in the postwar generation, and *A Thousand Days** (1965), the story of Kennedy in the White House. Both won Pulitzer Prizes. A more ambitious work, *The Age of Roosevelt** (3 vols., 1957-60), traced that President down to the 1936 election and left him there. His books are characterized by careful research and a superb writing style.

David Shannon (1920-   )

A Rutgers University professor specializing in recent American and labor history, Shannon has authored three fine books. *The Socialist Party of America** (1955) concludes that the party is dead. *The Decline of American Communism* (1959) is a first-rate narrative offering little interpretation. *Between the Wars: America, 1919-1941** (1965) is the finest interpretative treatment of the period. Highly readable, it exposes fallacious myths and clarifies complex matters admirably.

Kenneth Stampp (1912-   )

The University of California's Civil War and Reconstruction expert, Stampp has written three excellent books. *And the War Came* (1950) is a provocative, scholarly investigation of 1860 and 1861. *The Peculiar Institution** (1956) is the best one-volume treatment of slavery in the United States. It is written from the viewpoint of a civil rights worker seeking to discredit Ulrich Phillips, whose books he has supplanted. *The Era of Reconstruction** (1965) is a fine synthesis of research on the period, and like all his books, it is very readable.

Frederick Jackson Turner (1861-1932)

"The Significance of the Frontier in American History," a paper presented to the American Historical Association in 1893, has provoked more controversy than any other essay written on American history. Noting that the 1890 census had indicated there was no longer a front line of settlement, Turner sought to explain why the United States was so different from the European countries from which its people had come. He suggested that the frontier may well have contributed to the growth of democracy, hardy people, pragmatism, and nationalism. Though some of his followers made rather extravagant claims which have somewhat discredited Turner, the importance of the frontier is still being assessed today. His is surely one of the most important names in American historiography, although his list of publications is almost nonexistent.

Clarence Ver Steeg (1928-   )

Ver Steeg is Northwestern University's colonial historian. *The Formative Years, 1607-1763* (1964) is a fine survey of the colonial period, clearly and precisely written, but it does assume a certain basic knowledge of American history.

Walter Prescott Webb (1888-1963)

A disciple of Turner, a longtime professor at the University of Texas, and president of both the American Historical Association (1958) and the Mississippi Valley Historical Association (1953), Webb is most renowned for *The Great Plains** (1931). An original, thoughtful, suggestive work based on sound scholarship, it explores how the level, treeless, semi-arid conditions of the plains affected those who controlled them. *The Great Frontier* (1952) provoked much controversy as Webb sought parallels between the American, Australian, South African, and South American frontiers. Reaction varied from praise to the suggestion that he had carried the frontier thesis to its ultimate absurdity.

Bernard Weisberger (1922-   )

Weisberger wrote *Reporters for the Union* (1952), a well-researched but somewhat journalistic account. *They Gathered at the River** (1958) is a more substantial book, dealing with the revival movement as a uniquely American phenomenon. *The New Industrial Society** (1968) is a well-written survey of the last half of the nineteenth century, stressing the social adjustments forced by the changing economic and technological developments.

Thomas Jefferson Wertenbaker (1879-1966)

A Virginian who authored several books on his home state during his long professorship at Princeton, Wertenbaker is best remembered for his insightful, interpretive analysis of *The Puritan Oligarchy** (1947). His hostility to the Puritans contrasts him with many of the New Englanders writing of their own forebears; he felt that the failure of Puritanism's oligarchy to maintain itself was clear evidence of its shortcomings.

Robert Wiebe (1930-   )

A social historian at Northwestern, Wiebe has written two provocative books. *Businessmen and Reform** (1962) analyzes business attitudes toward Progressivism and concludes that business, far from being a united bloc against reforms, was fragmented into groups favoring (even initiating) and opposing reform legislation. *The Search for Order: 1877-1920** (1967) is a stimulating idea book which thoughtfully examines the social implications of urbanization and industrialization. Wiebe concludes that the most prominent characteristic of the period was the rise of a bureaucratic government to power. Both books are well written, but the latter is somewhat difficult for beginning students because of the abstract nature of much of the material. Wiebe has one of the most original historical minds on the present-day scene.

T. Harry Williams (1909-   )

A student of the Civil War and American military history teaching at Louisiana State, Williams has written *Lincoln and the Radicals** (1941), an ably done work which is perhaps too sympathetic to the President, and *Lincoln and His Generals** (1952), in which he argues for Lincoln's superior strategic grasp, not altogether convincingly. His writing is clear and fast-paced. His finest work is his Pulitzer Prize-winning biography of *Huey Long** (1969), unquestionably the best analysis of that colorful figure.

William Appleman Williams (1921-   )

A Marxist teaching at Oregon State, Williams has written several controversial volumes dealing with American history, including *The Contours of American History** (1961), a rather advanced book which advocates democratic socialism as the solution to the problems of society. *The Tragedy of American Diplomacy** (1962) criticizes American foreign policy since 1898 for its continued search for imperialist solutions to problems having their roots at home, and *The Roots of the Modern American Empire** (1969) pursues the criticism of American imperialism back to the Revolutionary War.

Harvey Wish (1909-   )

A longtime teacher at Western Reserve University, Wish wrote *Society and Thought in America* (2 vols., 1950-52), a readable, inclusive collection of facts with no conceptual framework holding them together. It is, even for a textbook, textbookish. *The American Historian* (1960) is an interesting treatment of the great American historians from a social-intellectual viewpoint. The prose is rather pedestrian though the book is quite good in parts.

C. Vann Woodward (1908-   )

The best of Dixie's interpreters, Woodward has written five outstanding books in his inimitable, smooth style. *Tom Watson: Agrarian Rebel** (1938) is one of the finest one-volume biographies about anyone. *Reunion and Reaction** (1951) is an economic interpretation of the Compromise of 1877, and full of insights. *The Origins of the New South, 1877-1913** (1951), a fresh view, is the most valuable book on the South in that period. *The Burden of Southern History** (1960) collects eight essays suggesting that the distinguishing element in Southern history is a common experience of poverty and defeat. *The Strange Career of Jim Crow** (1966) is a superb account of the history of segregation in the United States. Woodward belongs in the first rank of recent historians.

Louis B. Wright (1899-   )

As director of the Folger Shakespeare Library from 1948 to 1968, Wright brought a unique literary approach to his history writing. He is most noted for *The First Gentlemen of Virginia** (1940) and *The Cultural Life of the American Colonies, 1607-1763* (1957), a good treatment of literature, religion, and education in the colonies which becomes a bit monotonous in its detail.

Prominent World Historians

Raymond Aron (1905-   )

This brilliant Frenchman has written a number of forceful, analytic works with a sociological emphasis, but his most important book is *The Great Debate: Theories of Nuclear Strategy* (1965), perhaps the best treatment of the impact of thermonuclear weapons on military strategy and diplomacy. In all of his books the writing is succinct, precise, and tightly organized, making them very heavy reading. His stimulating mind has a humane, liberal bent reflected in his criticism of absolutist Marxian antipathy toward the West.

Maurice Ashley (1907-   )

This prolific English writer specializes in seventeenth-century England and has written three books about Oliver Cromwell, a fine text entitled *Great Britain to 1688* (1961), an entertaining volume on *The Stuarts in Love* (1964), and a large number of others. Though quite readable, Ashley tends to be cautious and avoid controversy. *The Greatness of Oliver Cromwell** (1957) is probably his finest book; it takes a sympathetic approach to the Puritan leader.

Roland Bainton (1894-   )

Born in England, this naturalized American citizen received his Ph.D. from Yale in 1921 and taught church history there until his retirement in 1962. His most important work is a biography of Martin Luther entitled *Here I Stand** (1950), an unbiased, candid, exciting, and highly readable book which remains the finest treatment of the Reformation leader.

Geoffrey Barraclough (1908-   )

This professor of modern history at Oxford specializes in German and English history, with his *The Origins of Modern Germany** (1946) and *The Medieval Papacy** (1968) standing out. In *An Introduction to Contemporary History** (1964) he offered the novel thesis that 1960 would in the future be regarded as the inauguration of contemporary times.

Bede (673-735)

Invariably referred to as the Venerable, he was the most learned man of his age, and in his *Ecclesiastical History of the English Nation** he became the first historian to date events from the birth of Christ.

James Henry Breasted (1865-1935)

America's leading Egyptologist, Breasted exerted a powerful influence as a translator and promoter of research in the area, particularly through his organizing the Oriental Institute at the University of Chicago in 1919. His books included *Ancient Records of Egypt* (5 vols., 1906), *History of Egypt** (1905), and *The Development of Religion and Thought in Ancient Egypt* (1912).

Crane Brinton (1898-1968)

This highly respected historian of forty-five years at Harvard wrote profound, generally readable books emphasizing the social and intellectual aspects of European history. His *Ideas and Men: The Story of Western Thought* (1950) is a lucid, stimulating treatment of the subject. *The Anatomy of Revolution** (1952), though not for the layman, is a brilliantly perceptive comparison of the English, American, French, and Russian revolutions. *A Decade of Revolution** (1934) remains one of the most popular titles in Harper's the Rise of Modern Europe series.

Geoffrey Bruun (1898-   )

This Canadian-born historian specializes in nineteenth-century history and published a survey of the period in 1959. His most important book is *Europe and French Imperium** (1938) in the Rise of Modern Europe series. Skillfully written, it analytically treats the age of Napoleon in a clear and stimulating style.

Alan Bullock (1914-   )

Bullock, the vice-chancellor of Oxford University since 1969, is renowned as a historian for his superb *Hitler: A Study in Tyranny** (1952). Unsurpassed as a treatment of the oft-described dictator, this unsensational, pleasingly written book is the standard against which all others are measured. Bullock has not matched that performance in his subsequent works.

Jacob Burckhardt (1818-1897)

A Swiss historian and writer on the Italian Renaissance, Burckhardt was termed the "wisest man of the nineteenth century" by Johan Huizinga. *The Civilization of the Renaissance in Italy** (1860), the first synthesis of the period, was a masterpiece. He also authored *The Age of Constantine the Great** (1853) and *Reflections on History* (1905), outlining his philosophy of history.

J. B. Bury (1861-1927)

Irish-born and educated, Bury taught for a quarter century at Cambridge. He wrote numerous first-rate histories of the Greek and Roman civilizations, and though his writing was rather heavy and austere, his research was very influential. In *The Idea of Progress** (1920) he summed up his philosophy: men are slowly advancing in a definite and desirable direction, and will continue to do so indefinitely since they will not soon reach the limits of their intelligence.

Herbert Butterfield (1900-   )

A distinguished British historian, Butterfield taught at Cambridge for twenty years and served three years as president of the Historical Association. He made his reputation with *The Whig Interpretation of History** (1931), and enhanced it with his *George III, Lord North, and the People* (1949), in which he explored the chaos of nonparty politics during the American

Revolution. Though he is not a brilliant writer, he has been thought provoking. *Christianity and History* (1949) is a compelling, scholarly argument for the case that meaning in history is found in Christianity.

Norman F. Cantor (1929-   )

A historian at Brandeis, Cantor specializes in medieval and English history. His *Medieval History: Life and Death of a Civilization* (1963) suggests that some moral order is necessary to prevent a society from sinking in chaos and despair. *The English** (1968), which received mixed reviews, treats constitutional development as the central theme of English history to 1760.

Thomas Carlyle (1795-1881)

This Scottish historian, author of biographies of Oliver Cromwell and Frederick the Great, is most famous for his basic interpretation of history. In *On Heroes, Hero-Worship, and the Heroic in History** (1841) he stated that "the history of the world is the biography of great men." Despite this belief, he devoted much attention to labor problems, the factory system, the failure of laissez faire, and other socio-economic subjects. He first established his reputation as a writer of the first rank with *The French Revolution** (1837), which is perhaps more admirable as literature than as history.

Edward Hallett Carr (1892-   )

A former British diplomat and Cambridge professor, E. H. Carr has written numerous volumes on twentieth-century European history. His balanced *The Twenty Years Crisis, 1919-1939** (1939) and *What Is History?** (1961), a liberal historian's analysis, are among his most important books. He has devoted most of his energy to *A History of Soviet Russia, 1917-1926** (8 vols., 1950–), a pragmatic in-depth analysis of the Russian revolution and its aftermath which despite its apparent impartiality is quite biased in favor of Lenin. Though an important work, it is a bit disappointing.

William Henry Chamberlin (1897-   )

From 1922 to 1935 the *Christian Science Monitor*'s correspondent in Russia, Chamberlain's major work is *The Russian Revolution, 1917-1921* (1935). It is a first-rate treatment of the subject, characterized by clarity, readability, and objectivity. The emphasis is factual rather than interpretative, but Chamberlin tends to sympathize with the counterrevolutionary movement, reflecting his disillusioned utopianism after his long stay in Soviet Russia.

Winston Churchill (1874-1965)

The great British statesman was also a noted historian. Among his most famous works are his biography of his ancestor *Marlborough** (4 vols., 1933-38), *A History of the English-Speaking Peoples** (4 vols., 1953-58), which tends to overemphasize politics and war, and *The Second World War** (6 vols., 1948-53). The latter shows off Chruchill's writing ability to best advantage; his sense of history and gift for language won him a Nobel Prize. Though he tends to magnify events in which he participated, and the work should be handled with some care for that reason, it is nonetheless a magnificent achievement.

Sir George Clark (1890-   )

This retired professor at Oxford and Cambridge specializes in seventeenth-century European history. His introductory volumes, *The Seventeenth Century** (1929) and *Early Modern Europe** (1957) are models of well-balanced scholarship. *The Later Stuarts* (1934) is an excellent impartial treatment of the subject.

Alfred Cobban (1901-1968)

Long a history professor at the University of London, Alfred Cobban specialized in modern French history. His *History of Modern France** (3 vols., 1957-65) is probably the best available. Bright and perceptive, his writing is a pleasure to read. He also took great interest in the Enlightenment, and his belief that the Age of Reason offers answers to many of today's problems indicates his rationalist bent.

George Douglas Howard Cole (1889-1959)

An Oxford professor, Cole wrote *The British People, 1746-1946** (rev. 1956), a history of radical movements within the working classes written from the viewpoint of a scholarly Socialist. His five-volume *A History of Socialist Thought* (1953) is an impressive, authoritative, and complete analysis of the thinkers of the movement, as opposed to the movement itself.

Thomas Costain (1885-1965)

Until 1945 the editor of various popular magazines, Costain spent the last twenty years of his life writing both fiction and nonfiction. His Pageant of England series (*The Conquering Family,** *The Magnificent Century,** *The Three Edwards,** and *The Last Plantagenets*)* offers the reader entertaining, personalized history. The books are written for a general readership and include created dialogue and simplified analysis of complex issues. They do offer a fairly accurate impression of the times, but occasionally the student in Costain is at odds with the novelist in him.

Gordon Craig (1913-   )

Educated at Princeton and teaching at Stanford, Gordon Craig is a specialist in German, military, and diplomatic history. *The Politics of the Prussian Army, 1640-1945** (1955) is a superbly written, well-documented treatment of German militarism. *War, Politics, and Diplomacy* (1966) includes fifteen perceptive essays on civil-military relations and other topics and offers valuable new insights into the area of Craig's expertise. He has also written *Europe Since 1815,* a fine, readable introductory text.

Benedetto Croce (1866-1952)

A highly influential Italian philosopher-historian, Croce held that history is an art form, and therefore subject to intuition and the creative impulse, an approach which did not produce good history. His four-volume *Philosophy of the Spirit* (1902-12) held that the mind or spirit is the sole reality and expressed itself through history. Though much of his writing was done during the Fascist period, his international prestige was so great that Mussolini dared not take action against his liberal views.

Philip Curtin (1922-   )

An African historian at the University of Wisconsin, Curtin wrote *The Image of Africa* (1964), a history of early nineteenth-century British ideas and attitudes toward Africa and Africans which gives evidence of considerable reflection on the complexities involved. *Africa Remembered** (1967) is a collection of ten personal narratives of the African side of slave-trading activity.

Will Durant (1885-   )

With a Ph.D. from Columbia, Will Durant launched his ten-volume *Story of Civilization* in 1935. Aided by his wife Ariel on the last four volumes, he completed the work to 1789 before deciding to stop in 1967, when *Rousseau and Revolution* (vol. X) won a Pulitzer Prize. His highly readable popular style, combined with his encyclopedic interest, indefatigable zest, good documentation, and humanistic approach make it one of the most popular treatments of world history. Written for the amateur rather than the professional, it tends to synthesize earlier writings.

Erik Erikson (1902-   )

A psychoanalyst, Erikson is primarily important to the history student for his inauguration of the psychoanalytic approach to history, most notably in his *Young Man Luther** (1958). This highly controversial volume, difficult to read, emphasizes Luther's relationship with his father and his identity crisis, dealing very little with the mature Luther. The student should be aware that Erikson's humanistic approach makes him incapable of understanding Luther's religious feeling. The book is not really a historical study, but a psychoanalytic one, and historians have debated with much vigor the validity of such an approach to the past.

John Donnelly Fage

An Englishman teaching at the University College of Ghana, Fage has co-authored *A Short History of Africa** (1963) with Roland Oliver, the best introduction to the subject for the student or layman. He has also written *Ghana: A Historical Interpretation** (1959), a brief introduction, and edited *Africa Discovers Her Past* (1970).

Merle Fainsod (1907-   )

How Russia Is Ruled (1953) is a comprehensive, scholarly treatment which is a basic guide to understanding Soviet rule. Fainsod delves into the differences in theory and practice, various instruments of control, and the impact of controls on factory and farm after analyzing the Bolshevik revolution.

John K. Fairbank (1907-   )

Since 1936 a Harvard professor and in 1968 president of the American Historical Association, John K. Fairbank is one of the most able American experts on China. His *The United States and China** (1948, rev. 1958), critical of Chiang, has had wide influence and is still probably the best synthesis on the subject. Though it is difficult to read, it offers a good perspective for the study of the present Chinese situation.

Sidney B. Fay (1876-1967)

A longtime Harvard professor, Sidney Fay is renowned for his two-volume *The Origins of the World War** (1928). In it he became the first American historian to attack the theory of Germany's sole guilt in the coming of the War. His good scholarship did much to win others to his point of view.

Michael T. Florinsky (1894-   )

A specialist on Russian totalitarianism, Florinsky is the editor of McGraw-Hill's *Encyclopedia of Russia and the Soviet Union* (1961) and the author of several histories of Russia. Probably the best is *Russia: A Short History* (1965), though *Toward an Understanding of the USSR* (1939), a two-volume work, is considerably more detailed.

Charles Patrick Fitzgerald (1902-   )

A professor at Australia's National University in Canberra, Fitzgerald is a leader in the field of Far Eastern history. He has written numerous books about China, generally stressing political and cultural affairs. Perhaps his finest volume is *The Birth of Communist China** (1965), a recent history which shows the depth of his background in Chinese history.

Pierre Gaxotte (1895-   )

This French journalist and biographer has written one of the best biographies of *Frederick II* (1938); in *Le Siècle de Louis XV* (1933), he tries to defend the reputation of an indefensible king. *The Age of Louis XIV* (trans. 1970), is a rather old-fashioned portrait not up to the standard of John Wolf's 1968 treatment.

Peter Gay (1923-   )

This Columbia University professor specializes in European intellectual history and political philosophy. His most noted work deals with the Enlightenment. *The Party of Humanity: Essays in the French Enlightenment** (1964) and *The Enlightenment: An Interpretation* (1966) both illustrate Gay's witty, erudite, smooth style and his humanistic, liberal approach to the movement with which he clearly sympathizes.

Leo Gershoy (1897-   )

A professor at New York University, Gershoy specializes in the French Revolution and eighteenth-century enlightened despotism. He has written two brief introductions to the French Revolution, as well as a superb biography—*Bertrand Barère: A Reluctant Terrorist* (1962). His *From Despotism to Revolution, 1763-1789** covers the pre-revolutionary period in the Rise of Modern Europe series.

Edward Gibbon (1737-1794)

Gibbon's *History of the Decline and Fall of the Roman Empire** is widely regarded as the greatest historical work ever written in English. It caused a sensation when it appeared because Gibbon, a militant agnostic, blamed the Christian church for the decline. Idealizing the political and intellectual freedom of classical literature, Gibbon felt Christianity had destroyed the classical culture. Despite various errors of fact and interpretation, the multi-volume work remains a classic of history and literature.

Charles Gibson (1920-   )

A specialist in colonial Latin American history, Gibson is a professor at the University of Michigan. In *The Aztecs under Spanish Rule* (1964) he offers a detailed look at the effect of Spanish institutions at the local level based on his own original research. *Spain in America* (1966) is an analytic and interpretive study of institutions and culture. He has written other fine books as well.

G. P. Gooch (1873-1968)

G. P. Gooch was a prolific writer—he authored over twenty-five books and co-edited others, including the *British Documents on the Origins of the War, 1898-1914*. Educated at Cambridge, he took an interest in all areas of modern European history. He wrote biographies of Frederick II, Louis XIV, Catherine the Great, Maria-Theresa, and Stanhope, among others, and an excellent *History of Modern Europe, 1878-1919* (1922). He is perhaps best known for his *History and Historians in the Nineteenth Century** (1913), a useful, interesting assessment of the profession in its infancy.

Elie Halévy (1870-1937)

A French historian, Halévy is the author of the classic *History of the English People in the Nineteenth Century* (6 vols., 1913-1946). It is the best detailed account of the subject, even though the 1852-1895 period was slighted. *England in 1815** is a particularly brilliant in-depth analysis of the state of the nation. Halévy was especially concerned with ideas (though not to the exclusion of events), particularly English nonconformity. He was the first to suggest the importance of Methodism in forestalling an English revolution.

John Hammond (1872-1949)

Along with his wife Barbara, John Hammond is famous for his many volumes on the social effects of the Industrial Revolution in England, most notably *The Rise of Modern Industry** (1925). Their interpretation is still widely held by the English people, but scholars are questioning its oversympathetic treatment of the victims of change. Colorfully and dramatically written, it is close to popular history despite its great accuracy.

Lewis Hanke (1905-   )

This Latin-American specialist has written a number of books treating all aspects of the area. Perhaps his two best are *The Spanish Struggle for Justice in the Conquest of America** (1949), a readable, well-documented re-evaluation of traditional concepts of the Spanish in America, and *Aristotle and the American Indians** (1958), a fascinating account of Spanish attempts to enslave the Indians according to Aristotle's belief that some races are naturally conditioned to be slaves. Hanke teaches at the University of California, Irvine.

Carlton J. H. Hayes (1882-1964)

A longtime professor at Columbia and a controversial Catholic diplomat in Spain during World War II, Hayes stimulated the study of nationalism at Columbia. He is probably best remembered for his contribution to the Rise of Modern Europe series, *A Generation of Materialism, 1871-1900** (1941). Neglecting no phase of European man's activities, that impartial, fair-minded volume is among the best in the entire series. The graceful writer authored some twenty-seven books on modern Europe and the Atlantic Community.

Hubert Herring (1889-1967)

Another Latin American expert, Herring authored one of the most popular texts on the area (rev. ed., 1961). He also wrote a well-received volume entitled *Good Neighbors* (1941), dealing mainly with the ABC powers and showing sympathy for the Latin American viewpoint. He taught at California's Claremont College.

Jack Hexter (1910-   )

A tough-minded dissenter and challenger of accepted historical truths, Hexter is most noted for *Reappraisals in History** (1961). Dealing primarily in English and European history, particularly in the early modern period, Hexter wittily and at times intemperately differs with those who would make the rise of the middle class the framework for modern European history. The Yale professor seeks to offer a more accurate view of society in the sixteenth and seventeenth centuries, and his ideas are widely debated.

Christopher Hill (1912-   )

Probably the foremost English authority on seventeenth-century English history, this Oxford professor is the author of a number of books on the period. *The Century of Revolution, 1603-1714** (1961) is probably the best survey of the century, brilliantly written and forcibly argued. *Puritanism and Revolution** (1958) is a masterful treatment of the subject, which the author has also explored in *The English Revolution, 1640* (1940), *Oliver Cromwell* (1958), and *The Intellectual Origins of the English Revolution* (1965), which attacks Puritanism as a myth. Hill's Marxist views should be kept in mind by the student—*The English Revolution,* arguing that the 1640 event was a clash between feudalism and capitalism, was written as a Marxist textbook, and all of Hill's books reflect an economic viewpoint.

Hajo Holborn (1902-1969)

German-born, a professor of history at Yale, and a past president of the American Historical Association (1967), Holborn was an outstanding authority on Germany. His three-volume *History of Modern Germany* (1959-69), despite lacking a bibliography and footnotes, is excellent. *The Political Collapse of Europe* (1951) is a brilliant brief treatment of European diplomacy since 1815. It argued for American recognition that World War I had destroyed the old political order and for the formulation of policies to suit the new reality.

H. Stuart Hughes (1916-   )

A Harvard professor specializing in the intellectual history of twentieth-century France, Germany, and Italy, Hughes is the author of *Contemporary Europe,* a text, and *Consciousness and Society** (1958). The latter, difficult but rewarding, treats European social thought from 1890 to 1930 and concludes that reason and emotion, the social sciences and literature, parted company in the twenties.

Johan Huizinga (1872-1945)

A Dutchman, Huizinga is most noted for his classic *The Waning of the Middle Ages** (1919), which has been translated into eight languages. The book studies the psychology and manner of the period just preceding the Renaissance in an original, thoughtful manner, suggesting that the civilization of the period was a reflection of the spirit of an age fleeing from reality into a beautiful dream.

Robert W. July (1918-   )

A professor at Hunter College, July is the author of *The Origins of Modern African Thought* (1968), a highly readable account of the development of society and thought in West Africa during the nineteenth and twentieth centuries.

Hans Kohn (1891-1971)

Czech-born in the crumbling Austro-Hungarian Empire, Kohn became an expert on nationalism, with *The Idea of Nationalism** (1944) becoming a standard work on the subject. He defined it as first and foremost a state of mind, an act of consciousness. He took a horizontal approach to the subject, distinguishing between Western and non-Western types, in contrast to Hayes' vertical, time-based analysis. Humanist and humanitarian, Kohn wrote in English with a grace, clarity, and elegance that belie his foreign origins.

William L. Langer (1896-   )

This unusually gifted diplomatic historian taught at Harvard from 1927 to 1964 and served as president of the American Historical Association in 1957. He is the editor of Harper's multi-volume Rise of Modern Europe series and an outstanding historian in his own right. He brilliantly unravelled the complexities of pre-war European diplomacy in *European Alliances and Alignments, 1871-1890* (1931) and *The Diplomacy of Imperialism, 1890-1902* (1935). After the Second World War he joined with S. Everett Gleason to author *The Challenge to Isolation* (1952) and *The Undeclared War* (1953), a superbly detailed account of the four years leading up to American entry in World War II. His writing is dense—there are no wasted words—and his books are long, but the quality is unsurpassed.

Ernest Lavisse (1842-1922)

This brilliant French historian, long a professor at the Sorbonne, left his most enduring monuments by editing a nineteen-volume history of France and co-editing a twelve-volume general history which is still regarded as a basic source in France.

George Lefebvre (1874-1959)

The most eminent twentieth-century historian of the French Revolution, Lefebvre has written numerous books on the subject, including *The Directory** (1946) and *The Thermidorians** (1937). His two-volume history of *The French Revolution** (trans. 1962-64) is a dispassionate, lucid account with a useful bibliography. Probably his best book is *The Coming of the French Revolution** (1947), the finest introduction to the Revolution and a work outstanding for its social analysis. His writing shows great learning and critical acumen, plus a fervent but undoctrinaire devotion to the Revolution.

Joseph R. Levenson (1920-1970)

A historian at Berkeley for twenty years before his accidental drowning, Levenson specialized in Chinese history. He co-authored *China: An Interpretive History* with Franz Schurmann in 1970. His greatest work was *Confucian China and Its Modern Fate** (3 vols., 1958-1965), a brilliant analytic intellectual history of modern China.

Thomas Babington Macaulay (1800-1859)
Author of a multi-volume history of England from 1688 to 1837, Macaulay is still a delight to read. The sweep of his work is perhaps second only to that of Gibbon, and his achievement is witnessed by the fact that it was translated into eleven languages. Despite his political partisanship (he gave up a political career to write), cocksure attitude, and lack of later scientific standards for material, his work is a classic. The emphasis is political and the outlook nationalistic.

Charles Howard McIlwain (1871-   )
A longtime constitutional historian at Harvard, McIlwain won a Pulitzer Prize for his constitutional interpretation of *The American Revolution** (1924). He wrote numerous other highly regarded books, including *The High Court of Parliament and Its Supremacy* (1910) and *The Growth of Political Thought in the West* (1932), which is a concisely reasoned, comprehensive account.

William H. McNeill (1917-   )
A broad thinker who has taken for his realm the history of the world, McNeill wrote *The Rise of the West** (1963), a fascinating and stimulating book stressing the interrelationships between various civilizations. In *A World History** (1967) he suggested that technological change is the propelling force in a mechanistic world. He teaches at the University of Chicago.

Alfred Thayer Mahan (1840-1914)
This important figure wrote two books which had great impact on European and American naval policy: *The Influence of Sea Power Upon History, 1660-1783** (1890) and *The Influence of Sea Power Upon the French Revolution and Empire, 1793-1812* (2 vols., 1892). His popularity in England, Germany, and the United States did much to stimulate a naval building race on the

eve of World War I, and the admiral's opinions carried great weight with Theodore Roosevelt, a historian in his own right.

Frederic William Maitland (1850-1906)

This great English historian, ranked by some with Gibbon and Macaulay, brought historical methods to bear upon the development of English law and legal institutions in a number of authoritative works. His clear, vigorous style and his mastery of English legal history, combined with his scholarly qualities, made him one of the giants of the historical field.

Friedrich Meinecke (1862-1954)

A German historian only recently available in English translation, Meinecke wrote two outstanding books treating German political thought. *Cosmopolitanism and the National State* is an innovative, indispensable portrayal of German thought in the eighteenth and nineteenth centuries. *Machiavellism* treats the vital factor of "necessity of state" and its critical influence on modern history.

Barrington Moore, Jr.

A senior research fellow at Harvard's Russian Research Center, Barrington Moore has written a profoundly important book: *Social Origins of Dictatorship and Democracy: Lord and Peasant in the Making of the Modern World** (1966). In it he explores English, French, American, Japanese, Chinese, and Indian societies to see why some have become democratic and others fascist or communist. He concludes that the peasantry is the central facet of revolution, escaping Marxist orthodoxy and its requirement of bourgeois revolution. Moore is exceptionally perceptive and at the same time not afraid to discuss ideas which he has come to reject.

George Mosse (1918-   )

A specialist in European intellectual history at the University of Wisconsin, Mosse has written several books. Most noteworthy is the controversial *Crisis of German Ideology** (1964) in which he sought to examine the roots of Naziism and concluded that it was neither an aberration nor latent in other cultures, but was specifically in the German tradition dating back to romanticism. The German-born Mosse assumes some knowledge of German on the reader's part.

Sir Lewis Namier (1888-1960)

This Russian-born British subject gained his fame as a revisionist historian of eighteenth-century English politics, most notably with his *England in the Age of the American Revolution* * (1930). He used the behavioral approach to attempt an explanation of why Parliament acted as it did, applying the tools of the behavioral school of political science to his study of the period. He concluded that despite the presence of a Whig and Tory "mentality" in the 1760s, there were no organized parties in the modern sense. He also wrote *The Structure of Politics at the Accession of George III* * (1929).

John E. Neale (1890-   )

A longtime professor at the University of London, Neale is the outstanding authority on politics in Elizabethan England. His biography *Queen Elizabeth* * (1934), a first-rate literary work, was translated into eight languages. He is most renowned in historical circles for his excellent research in Elizabethan parliamentary history. *The Elizabethan House of Commons* (1949) and his two-volume *Elizabeth I and Her Parliaments* * (1953, 1957) are masterpieces of research, writing, and interpretation.

Harold Nicolson (1886-1968)

An English political figure and diplomat, Nicolson was the very image of the British Foreign Office. Among his earlier works are his excellent first-person *Peacemaking 1919* * (1933) and the highly readable, well-proportioned *The Congress of Vienna* * (1946). In the future he may be best remembered for his superb *Diaries and Letters* (3 vols., 1966-68), a fascinating account of his career which indulges freely in speculation about what might have been, paints brilliant character portraits, and irresistably draws one back into the period being discussed.

Roland A. Oliver (1923-   )

Oliver, a professor at the University of London, co-authored *A Short History of Africa** (1962) with J. D. Fage and has edited four other collections on African history. His most useful specialized work is *The Missionary Factor in East Africa** (1952), a fascinating account of missionary activity in Uganda, Kenya, and Tanganyika.

R. R. Palmer (1909-   )

A Princeton professor specializing in eighteenth-century history and particularly the French Revolution, Palmer served as president of the American Historical Association in 1970. His most notable work is *The Age of the Democratic Revolution* (2 vols., 1959, 1964), an important study in which he searched for the common ideas and situations in the American Revolution and its European counterparts. It is a major work of synthesis and interpretation which has found great favor with the critics.

Sir Bernard Pares (1867-1949)

This Englishman was a frequent visitor to Russia in the years preceding World War I. When the Communists allowed him back in 1936, be aroused their ire by saying they would not endure in their present form for they had actually ceased practicing communism. His *History of Russia** (1926) is a classic, but *The Fall of the Russian Monarchy* (1939) is his best work. An authoritative account for the historian and the general reader, it is a basic source for the period.

Henri Pirenne (1862-1935)

This renowned Belgian historian, author of a seven-volume economically oriented *Histoire de Belgique,* is probably most famous today for the "Pirenne thesis" that the break between antiquity and the Middle Ages was not in the fifth century but around 700, when the Muslims conquered the southern shore of the Mediterranean. The theory, based on economic considerations, has aroused heated controversy.

J. H. Plumb (1911-   )

A specialist in eighteenth-century England at Cambridge, Plumb has written *The First Four Georges** (1956), *Chatham* (1953), and *The Growth of Political Stability in England, 1675-1725* (1967). His greatest undertaking was *Sir Robert Walpole* (2 vols., 1956, 1960), a dense, heavy reading, objective biography of the first prime minister. Despite Plumb's vigorous style, it is difficult reading.

Albert F. Pollard (1869-1948)

Long a professor at the University of London, founder of the Institute of Historical Studies in London, author of *A Short History of the Great War* (1920), one of the first and clearest one-volume treatments of the conflict, and many other volumes, Pollard will perhaps best be remembered as an assistant editor of the *Dictionary of National Biography*, to which he contributed some 500 articles, the equivalent of one volume.

William H. Prescott (1796-1859)

This New England Unitarian devoted most of his life to writing about the golden colonial years of Spain, the conquest of Mexico and Peru, Ferdinand, Isabella, and Phillip II. His work is something of a historical and literary landmark in the United States.

Leopold von Ranke (1795-1886)

The giant of nineteenth-century German historical work, Ranke was the first to establish the historical seminar which has had such great influence in England and the United States. A rebel against the utilitarian moralism of the Enlightenment, Ranke saw links between Christianity and humanist cultural values and believed that the Christian God ruled over world history. Perhaps his greatest legacy was his conquest of historical relativism through a personal blending of knowledge and belief. Lord Acton called him "almost the Columbus of modern history."

John Reed (1887-1920)

A journalist and poet most noted for creating the Communist Labor Party in the United States in 1919, Reed wrote a number of books. *Ten Days That Shook the World** (1919) is a vivid, dramatic, minutely detailed account of the November revolution in Russia. Considering Reed's bias, the book is reasonably objective. Its status is evident from the fact that Lenin wrote the introduction to a later edition.

Edwin O. Reischauer (1910-   )

A longtime Harvard professor of East Asian studies, Reischauer served as Ambassador to Japan from 1961 to 1966. He has written *Japan Past and Present* (1946) and *The United States and Japan** (rev. 1965), a reliable, readable work which is basic to the study of relations between the two. *Beyond Vietnam: The United States and Asia** (1967) argues convincingly that the United States should use economic and political power rather than military strength to win popular support for Saigon, then explores the whole range of American relations in the Far East.

Pierre Renouvin (1893-   )

The dean of French diplomatic historians, Renouvin is the author of two highly recommended works on diplomacy in the twentieth century: *War and Aftermath, 1919-1929* (1968) and *World War II and Its Origins: International Relations, 1929-45* (1968). Though containing few surprises, they provide a fine introduction to the subject and include extensive bibliographies.

J. Fred Rippy (1892-   )

This longtime Latin American expert at the University of Chicago has written many books on the region, particularly emphasizing foreign relations in such works as *The United States and Mexico* (1926) and *Latin America in World Politics* (1928). His best work is *Latin America: A Modern History* (rev. 1968) in the University of Michigan series. Clear, concise, and well-documented, the book is far more interpretive than most texts, and stresses international relations, particularly in the realm of economics.

Gerhard Ritter (1888-   )

A former member of the German resistance, Ritter has written a distinguished and penetrating study of that movement: *The German Resistance: Carl Goerdeler's Struggle Against Tyranny* (1959). As a defense of the resistance it offers a corrective to Wheeler-Bennett's *Nemesis of Power,* and as such is rather controversial. The English translation, unfortunately, is abridged.

J. H. Rose (1855-1942)

This Englishman made his major contributions shortly after the turn of the century with his popular *Life of Napoleon I* (1901) and his two-volume biography of William Pitt (1911-12), probably still the most authoritative treatment of that prime minister.

Sir George Sansom (1883-   )

An Englishman and a longtime official in the British embassy in Tokyo, Sansom is the outstanding Western authority on Japanese history. *Japan: A Short Cultural History* (1931) is the best treatment of that subject, stressing economic, social, and religious factors over political ones. *The Western World and Japan* (1950) is a superb account supplementing the former for the period to 1894. His three-volume *History of Japan** (1958-63) takes the story to 1867, and is a masterpiece. Like all his work, it combines a graceful style, superb scholarship, and penetrating analysis.

H. Franz Schurmann (1926-   )

A specialist in Chinese history teaching at Berkeley, Schurmann co-authored *China: An Interpretive History* (1970), a rather abstract advanced history. His own finest work is *Ideology and Organization in Communist China** (1969), a stimulating sociological approach of considerable influence based in large part on personal observation.

Hugh Seton-Watson (1916-   )

The University of London's expert on Eastern Europe and Russia, Seton-Watson has written a number of distinguished volumes. The most important of these, since they treat an area so neglected, are *Eastern Europe Between the Wars** (1945), a penetrating, comprehensive, and indispensable analysis stressing the psychological and social tendencies of the various countries, and *The East European Revolution** (1950), a scholarly analysis of the postwar transformation of the region.

William L. Shirer (1904-   )

An American journalist in Berlin from 1934 to 1941, Shirer published the absorbing *Berlin Diary** in 1941. In 1960 he completed his monumental *The Rise and Fall of the Third Reich,** an excellent political and military history of the Nazis which offers few new insights but is fascinating reading and a must for history students. *The Collapse of the Third Republic** (1970) is a dramatic, scholarly treatment of the moral collapse of France in 1939 and 1940.

Preserved Smith (1880-1941)

Preserved Smith wrote two important books. *The Age of the Reformation** (1920), sympathetic to the Protestant viewpoint, ranks him as one of the foremost experts on the period. It includes a sixty-seven page bibliography. *A History of Modern Culture** (2 vols., 1930-34) is a clear, solid description of the 1543-1776 period. It is more workmanlike than interpretative.

Edgar Snow (1905-1972)

This American writer was the Westerner closest to Mao Tse-tung. His *Red Star Over China** (1937), critical of Chiang and sympathetic to the Communists, is the best account of the thirties there, offering a good description of life among the Communists and biographical accounts of the leadership. *The Other Side of the River* (1962) is a sympathetic account of Red China which suggests that the United States should court the Far Eastern giant. Though the idea was very controversial in

1962, President Nixon was preparing for his trip to Peking when Snow died.

Raymond Sontag (1897-   )

Long a distinguished diplomatic historian at Berkeley, Sontag wrote the popular *European Diplomatic History, 1871-1932* (1933), a clear, scholarly text, and the interpretative and intriguing *Germany and England: Background of Conflict, 1848-1894** (1938). He also served as American editor-in-chief of *Documents on German Foreign Policy, 1918-1945.*

Oswald Spengler (1880-1936)

The Decline of the West (1923), translated into six languages, was this German's major work. It enjoyed huge success through its appeal to an era of misery and despair. The thesis is that history is cyclic, that dominant races go through stages of youth, growth, maturity, and decline like people, and that Western civilization was about to decline. Spengler believed Asians would provide the next hegemonic race.

Sir Leslie Stephen (1832-1904)

This rationalist edited the first twenty-six volumes of the *Dictionary of National Biography* and also contributed *The English Utilitarians* (1900) to British intellectual history. His best work was his *History of English Thought in the Eighteenth Century** (1876), a superbly written, learned work reflecting his rationalist views.

Lytton Strachey (1880-1932)

Variously described as one of the great writers of all time and a collector of trivialities, Strachey is most famous for his *Eminent Victorians** (1918) and *Queen Victoria** (1921). His style is acidly ironic and brings his subjects very much alive; reading his books is a stimulating experience.

Frank Tannenbaum (1893-   )

Long a Latin American specialist at Columbia, Tannenbaum earned fame for his brief *Slave and Citizen: The Negro in the*

Americas* (1947). Though criticized as one-sided (sympathetic to the Negro), far from profound, and poorly executed, it served as a stimulus to the comparative approach to the study of slavery.

R. H. Tawney (1880-1962)

A Fabian Socialist advocating the socialization of the economic system, Tawney spent some time as professor of economic history at the University of London. He gained fame with *The Acquisitive Society** (1920) and added greatly to it with *Religion and the Rise of Capitalism** (1926). In the latter he showed how revolutionary Christian social theory was and expounded Max Weber's thesis that Calvinism was instrumental in the rise of capitalism. Profound, brilliant, impartial, and beautifully written, the book is a classic.

A. J. P. Taylor (1906-   )

One of England's finest historians, Taylor specializes in diplomatic history. *The Struggle for Mastery in Europe, 1848-1918** (1954) is a superb account of the last days of the European balance of power which includes a thirty-page critical bibliography. *The Origins of the Second World War** (1961) is a sensational account which suggests that Hitler did not want war, but rather a peaceful revision of Versailles. In this account there are no heroes and no villains, which is particularly surprising in light of Taylor's reputation as being anti-German. Like all his writing, these two books are witty, stimulating, and a pleasure to read.

E. P. Thompson (1924-   )

Thompson has written the most important book on English labor since the Hammonds' work. A far-leftist, he is intensely sympathetic to the working class. His humane imagination and controlled passion bring alive the early nineteenth century and challenge many kinds of contemporary orthodoxy. *The Making of the English Working Class** (1963) is a controversial masterpiece.

Leonard M. Thompson (1916-   )

Thompson is probably the ranking expert on the history of the Union of South Africa, having authored three books on the subject. The best is his *Unification of South Africa, 1902-1910* (1960), a lucid, superbly organized, painstakingly researched book which will long be the standard work on the subject. It is graced by an excellent bibliography.

John Toland (1912-   )

This nonacademic author of popular history has two titles of importance in print. *The Last 100 Days** (1966), based on recent interviews with participants, details the last three months of World War II in Europe in a stimulating, entertaining style. *The Rising Sun** (1970) moves to the Pacific front, offers a superb analysis of the Japanese mind, and traces in too much detail the decline and fall of the Japanese Empire after 1936.

Arnold Toynbee (1889-   )

Toynbee is the author of *A Study of History** (10 vols., 1934-54), a work which ranks with Gibbon's and Spengler's as intellectual history. His thesis is that civilizations grow by responding successfully to challenges under the leadership of creative minorities, and decline when the leaders fail to respond creatively. Unlike Spengler, he does not regard the death of a civilization as inevitable. He regards history as shaped by spiritual rather than economic forces, and has been criticized for being more a Christian moralist than a historian. His lack of Anglocentrism contrasts strikingly with Spengler's focus on Germany. While some historians challenge these and others of his views, his greatness is secure. The poetic vision of his work and his sense of the vast continuity of history combine to make his work a classic.

G. M. Trevelyan (1876-1962)

A traditional English liberal historian and longtime teacher at Cambridge, Trevelyan believed that the same book should appeal to the general reader and to the scholar; as a result, his writing is very colorful. Though his work was not particularly original, it was invariably of high quality. A few of his vast number of titles are *England Under the Stuarts** (1905), *Lord Grey of the Reform Bill* (1920), and *A History of England** (1926).

H. R. Trevor-Roper (1914-   )

A rather controversial English historian, Trevor-Roper wrote *The Gentry, 1540-1640* (1953) in which he suggested that contrary to Tawney's belief, the English revolution was caused by the decline of part of the gentry. The debate thus begun continues even today. *The Rise of Christian Europe** (1965), a colorful and exciting book, is also provocative and some of Trevor-Roper's interpretations have come under fire. He won his first fame with *The Last Days of Hitler** (1947), which had quite wide appeal.

Leon Trotsky (1877-1940)

Trotsky's three-volume *History of the Russian Revolution* (1932-33), a manual on how to make a revolution, is the most important study of the subject. Not only is it good history and good literature, but it has been rated a work of art and one of the most important books of the century. Obviously Trotsky is not objective, but his first-hand account is surprisingly judicious. It marks Trotsky as an accomplished historian.

Tang Tsou

Born in China, this naturalized American citizen specializes in recent Chinese history. His finest volume is *America's Failure in China, 1941-1950** (1963), which is critical of both the American left and right. His profound analysis concludes that Chiang's frailties were fatal to the nationalist cause, for Chiang placed loyalty to himself above competence and integrity in his subordinates. It is a first-rate volume.

Barbara Tuchman (1912-   )

A remarkably gifted writer, Barbara Tuchman has written three historical best sellers. *The Guns of August** (1962), winner of a Pulitzer Prize, brilliantly treats the opening

days of World War I in great depth. *The Proud Tower**
(1966) offers unforgettable portraits of various aspects of
society in the generation before the war. *Stilwell and the
American Experience in China, 1911-1945* (1970), acclaimed
as her finest book, uses Stilwell as a vehicle for her discussion
of Sino-American relations for the period. Using proper
historical method, enormous research, and a colorful pen,
Mrs. Tuchmann, like Trevelyan, writes for both the scholar
and the general reader.

George Vernadsky (1887-   )

For thirty years a Russian historian at Yale, Vernadsky is the
most prolific student of Russia in America. Erudite and ener-
getic, he wrote in the grand historical style of the nineteenth
century. His five-volume history of Russia, written from 1943 to
1969 and carrying the story up to 1682 (others are to finish the
story in a total of ten volumes), embodies his agreeable style
and detailed and penetrating analysis.

Theodore H. von Laue (1916-   )

A naturalized American citizen, the German-born von Laue is a
professor at Washington University in St. Louis. His most noted
book is *Why Lenin? Why Stalin?** (1964), which suggests that
much of the significance of the Russian Revolution is to be
found in a nationalistic desire to replace the West as the model
for emerging nations. His graceful style and fresh approach
make the book useful for both the scholar and the general
reader.

Barbara Ward (1914-   )

More an economist than an historian, Barbara Ward has written
numerous books stressing the gap between the developed and
undeveloped nations of the world. Most famous of those, and
reportedly President Kennedy's favorite book, is *The Rich
Nations and the Poor Nations** (1962), which calls upon the
rich to help the poor—or face the consequences. Somewhat
more historical is her *Five Ideas that Change the World** (1959).

Max Weber (1864-1920)

This German sociologist, political economist, and political writer introduced the suggestion that Calvinism was responsible for the rise of capitalism. In *The Protestant Ethic and the Spirit of Capitalism** (trans. 1930) he noted that Calvinists regarded material success as a sign of God's favor and were thus inspired to develop a capitalistic spirit. R. H. Tawney is also associated with this thesis.

Sir Charles K. Webster (1886-1961)

A model scholar, Webster wrote four outstanding books about British diplomatic history in the early nineteenth century. His two finest trace *The Foreign Policy of Castlereagh* from 1812 to 1822. Massive research coupled with a background in diplomacy make his judicious accounts splendid examples of historical presentation.

C. V. Wedgewood (1910-   )

A specialist in seventeenth-century history, Ms. Wedgewood wrote *The Thirty Years War** (1938), one of the best short histories of the subject. It is interestingly written, objective, and full of fresh interpretation. Perhaps more famous is her two-volume treatment of the English Revolution, *The King's Peace, 1637-1641** (1955) and *The King's War, 1641-1647* (1958), which contains a wealth of material beyond that suggested by the titles.

H. G. Wells (1866-1946)

Though primarily a novelist, this Englishman sold over two million copies of his *Outline of History,* a rationalist, materialist approach to world history which held that man could progress only if he adapted himself to his changing environment.

Alexander Werth (1901-1969)

A Russian-born British citizen, Werth as a journalist and author has written numerous books on twentieth-century France and Russia. Among the finest are *France 1940-1945** (1956), translated into nine languages, and *DeGaulle** (1965), a political biography which is highly readable and paints the United States as the villain of the piece. *Russia at War 1941-45** (1964) is a massive book focusing on the human side of war. Written more as journalism than history, it is interesting reading.

Sir John W. Wheeler-Bennett (1902-   )

A superb writer and the leading authority on German history from 1918 to 1945, Wheeler-Bennett has authored several very important books. *Hindenburg: The Wooden Titan** (1936) is the most authoritative biography of that figure. *Munich: Prologue to Tragedy** (1948) is a vivid example of classic diplomatic history and an outstanding treatment of the Munich agreement. *Nemesis of Power: The German Army in Politics, 1918-1945** (1953) explores all the tragic implications of military involvement in government and leaves the reader with a moral.

Basil Willey (1897-   )

An English scholar with a lucid, urbane literary style, Willey specializes in British intellectual history. His three books on the subject form a trilogy: *The Seventeenth-Century Background** (1934), *The Eighteenth-Century Background* (1940), and *Nineteenth-Century Studies** (1949, with a second volume in 1956). Willey traces the struggles between religion and science as the central theme of the books.

Bertram Wolfe (1896-   )

This fine historian of Russia has written numerous books. His *Three Who Made a Revolution** (1948) is a classic about Lenin, Trotsky, and Stalin. *Marxism: One Hundred Years in the Life of a Doctrine** (1965) is a brilliant analysis of the conflicting claims of revolutionary Leninists and democratic socialists to Marxist orthodoxy. Wolfe concludes that the contradictory impulses in Marx himself betrayed his followers as industrial nations did not have revolutions.

Gordon Wright (1912-   )

Specializing in modern European history and particularly that of France, this Stanford professor has authored a number of fine books, including *The Reshaping of French Democracy** (1948) and *France in Modern Times, 1760-1960* (1960). Perhaps his best book is *The Ordeal of Total War, 1939-1945** (1968), in which he explores the economic, psychological, and scientific dimensions of World War II.

Glossary of Historical Terms

Absolutism. A political theory that absolute power should be vested in one or more rulers, as contrasted with limited power under a constitutional system.

Ambassador. A diplomatic agent of the highest rank.

Anarchism. A political theory holding all forms of governmental authority to be unnecessary and undesirable and advocating a society based on cooperation and free association of individuals and groups. Commonly involves violence.

Ante Bellum. Latin term for the period before a war.

Appeasement. Diplomatic policy of giving in to strong demands from a powerful nation in order to avert the possibility of war.

Arbitration. The settlement of a dispute between nations by a person or group mutually selected by the disputants for that purpose.

Archives. A place in which public records or historical documents are preserved.

Aristocracy. A privileged upper class, or nobility, which is possessed of political, social, and economic rights not accorded to the mass of the people. Normally hereditary.

Armistice. Temporary suspension of hostilities by agreement between the two sides. Usually the forerunner of a peace treaty, whereas a truce is merely a temporary cessation.

Autonomy. Self-governing or independent status for a nation-state.

Balance of Power. An equilibrium of power between two or more nations sufficient to prevent any one from becoming strong enough to make war or otherwise attempt to impose its will upon another.

Belligerent. A nation which is engaging in war and is legally recognized as such by several or all other nations.

Benevolent Despot. An absolute ruler whose goal is the welfare of his subjects.

Blockade. A restrictive measure designed to obstruct the commerce and communications of an unfriendly nation by military and naval means.

Bourgeoisie. The middle class, generally socially and politically associated with private property interests.

Buffer State. An independent nation or territory strategically located between potential belligerent powers and acting as security for one or both powers against attack.

Canon Law. The rules and regulations of a religious organization, most often used with reference to the Catholic Church.

Capitalism. An economic system based on private property ownership, the wage system, individual initiative, competition, and the profit motive.

Causus belli. Latin term for the causes or justification for going to war.

Clericalism. A political system which upholds the power of a religious hierarchy.

Collective Security. The maintenance by common action of the security of all members of an association of nations.

Communism. Theoretically, an economic system based on public ownership of the means of production, with profits being shared by all members of the society, and eventually resulting in the abolition of class and government. In practice, usually results in totalitarianism and lack of freedom.

Conciliarism. The movement in the Catholic Church since the Middle Ages holding that a general church council is superior to the Pope.

Confederation. A political organization consisting of a union of sovereign political bodies for specific purposes only, with real power residing in the member nations. Contrast with federation.

Conservatism. A political philosophy based on tradition and social stability, stressing established institutions, and preferring gradual development to abrupt change. Tends to stress order above freedom.

Constitutionalism. Government based on an agreement between the people and their rulers, either written or unwritten, establishing the limits of power and the duties of that government.

Contraband. Material belligerents consider necessary to their war effort. Contraband articles on neutral ships may be seized by belligerents if they are destined for enemy nations.

Coup d'etat. The violent overthrow or alteration of a government by a small group.

Convention. A treaty of a specific nature which is usually agreed to by many nations concurrently.

Darwinism. The theory of evolution which holds that creatures survive and improve by adapting to environmental changes. Also known as natural selection or survival of the fittest.

De facto. Pertains to a government which actually exists, but which is not yet recognized as legitimate or stable by other established nations.

De jure. Pertains to any government recognized as legitimate by other nations, even though it may not actually be functioning (such as a government in exile during a war).

Depression. A period in a business cycle marked by lower wages, unemployment, and declining profits. A recession is a relatively mild depression.

Dominion. A self-governing nation of the British Commonwealth other than the United Kingdom that acknowledges the British monarch as chief of state.

Dynasty. The hereditary ruling family of a nation. Also the name given to the historical period when a particular ruling house held power.

Embargo. Trade restrictions placed by a nation on international commerce. Usually employed as a coercive measure. May pertain to a single nation or commodity.

Entente. An international understanding providing for a common course of action.

Evolution. Gradual change, as contrasted to revolution, or sudden change.

Extraterritoriality. The right or privilege of a person to be tried under his own legal system even when residing on alien territory.

Fascism. A totalitarian, capitalistic governmental system which glorifies nationalism, militarism, and racism, while suppressing individual liberties. Its major difference from totalitarian communism is the presence of a capitalistic economic system.

Federation. A union of sovereign political bodies which give up most or all of their sovereignty to create an overriding superior governing body of permanent stature.

Feudalism. The system of political organization in medieval Europe whereby individuals held land and political power from their rulers in exchange for political support and military service.

Freedom of the Seas. The right of a merchant ship to travel any except territorial waters either in peace or war.

Free Ships Make Free Goods. The international theory that the nonmilitary goods of a belligerent are free from seizure by other belligerents when being transported on vessels of a neutral nation.

Free Trade. Trade based on the unrestricted international exchange of goods with tariffs used only as a source of revenue.

Gentlemen's Agreement. An understanding between national leaders the enforcement of which rests on the good will of the parties involved.

Good Offices. An attempt to bring quarreling nations together, though without any proposition to resolve the quarrel.

Guild System. Medieval organization of individuals employed in a certain craft to establish training requirements, business practices, and mutual protection of the members.

Heretic. A person who upholds doctrines which are opposed to the official teachings of a religious body. Heresy is any teaching which runs contrary to the official teachings of such a body.

Holding Company. A business organization created to hold the stocks of many producing companies in order to control the prices and behavior of these companies in the direction of monopoly.

Iconoclasm. The policy of attacking and destroying the traditional venerated objects, institutions, and doctrines of a religious body.

Imperialism. That policy engaged in by a nation which seeks to expand the political and/or economic control of the nation at the expense of other weaker nations.

Impressment. The policy of strong navy nations forcibly to press individuals into naval service, often by removing them from the vessels of other nations.

Insurgency. A condition of revolt against a government that is less than an organized revolution and is not recognized as belligerency.

International Law. Those principles which a majority of civilized nations agree to respect in their intercourse with one another.

Isolationism. The policy of a nation to avoid any entangling dealings with other nations. Contrast with internationalism.

Jingoism. Sword-rattling—a militant, warlike stand in foreign policy.

Letter of Marque. The official written sanction by a government to private individuals empowering them to engage in privateering, which means attacking enemy shipping at their own expense and sharing the profits with the government. ment.

Liberalism. An individual or governmental attitude which favors changes in the existing structure to further individual freedom. In the past this meant limiting governmental intervention in private affairs. In the twentieth century it has come to mean greater governmental power to provide basic services for the people.

Mandate. Territory governed by an advanced nation at the request and sanction of a governing body of nations.

Manor. The territories held by a lord from his king, over which he exercises authority and subdivides the land into parcels to be worked by his serfs—the economic side of feudalism.

Mediation. The nonbinding suggestion of a solution to a quarrel between two other nations.

Mercantilism. A political-economic theory whereby a nation seeks self-sufficiency through the accumulation of gold and silver by means of a favorable balance of trade and by colonies for raw materials and markets.

Mercenary. A professional soldier who sells his services to the army of any nation for monetary compensation.

Mobilization. To ready the armed forces of a nation for battle. Usually a rather lengthy process, it was regarded as an agressive measure.

Modus vivendi. A temporary agreement between nations which is only in force until a final settlement is reached.

Monasticism. Pertains to the system in which religious men and women retire from the world to a cloistered existence in a monastery, nunnery, or convent, and live a permanent, communal religious life.

Monograph. An article or a book written about one specific subject only.

Moratorium. A legally authorized period of delay in the performance of a legal obligation or the payment of a debt.

Most-favored-nation Theory. Agreement between two nations which states that they will give no other nation greater commercial privileges than they grant to each other.

Nationalism. Loyalty and devotion to a nation, particularly in the sense of placing the national interest above that of other nations of supranational groups.

Neutrality. The diplomatic state of being neutral, which under international law assures immunity from invasion or use by belligerents.

Oligarchy. Government by the few.

Open Door. A policy giving opportunity for commercial intercourse with a country to all nations on equal terms.

Pacifism. Opposition to war or violence as a means of settling disputes, including refusal to bear arms on moral or religious grounds.

Papal Bull. A formal pronouncement on the teachings and interpretations of the Catholic Church as formulated by the Pope.

Paper Blockade. A declared blockade which is nonenforceable due to a lack of sufficient military strength. Usually not considered binding by other nations.

Parity. An equivalence between farmers' current purchasing power and their purchasing power at a selected base period. In military terminology, a balance of power with one's rival nation.

Patronage. The power on the part of a politician to appoint various individuals to public offices, usually as a reward for political support.

Plagiarism. To steal or present as one's own an idea or passage derived from an existing source.

Plebiscite. A vote by which the people of an entire country or district express an opinion for or against a proposal, frequently used to determine independent status or choice of government.

Post bellum. Latin term for the period immediately following a war.

Pragmatism. A philosophical system which assesses the validity of an idea by whether or not it actually works. Tends to result in relative morality.

Primary source. A firsthand source of information, such as a letter, a diary, or an interview giving the words of the witnesses or first recorders of an event.

Primogeniture. The feudalistic European practice of the father's estate being passed on undivided to the eldest son, to prevent the fragmentation of political and economic power.

Progressivism. The favoring of progress through a program of social and political reform.

Protective tariff. Import duties which are sufficiently high to limit the importation of foreign goods, thereby protecting domestic industry from foreign competition.

Protectorate. A weak or small nation over which a strong nation assumes protection, usually concerning foreign affairs, and usually with some strings attached.

Provisional Government. A temporary government established to provide law and order pending the final determination of a permanent form of government, frequently necessary immediately following a revolution.

Rapprochement. Establishment of cordial relations.

Ratification. Formal approval or sanction of an act of government by the proper consenting authority.

Reactionary. An extreme conservative inclined toward a former political or social order or policy.

Reciprocity. The granting of favorable commercial benefits to a nation with the condition that the other nation respond in equal manner.

Reconstruction. The process of rebuilding an area or a nation following a devastating war.

Reparations. Compensation in money or materials payable by a defeated nation for damages to or expenditures sustained by another nation as a result of hostilities with the defeated nation.

Revenue Tariff. Import duties sufficiently low so as not to curtail the importation of foreign goods, but rather to obtain revenues from the duties imposed on the goods.

Revolution. A fundamental change in political organization, especially the overthrow or renunciation of one government or ruler and the substitution of another by the governed.

Schism. The disunion of an organized group (society, church, political party) because of differences of opinion on basic doctrines or beliefs.

Secondary source. One produced by the historian through the utilization of a number of primary, or firsthand, sources.

Self-determination. The right of the people residing in a given area to determine for themselves their form of government.

Shirt-sleeve Diplomacy. Informal diplomacy.

Socialism. An economic system which calls for public ownership and operation of the means of production, the sharing of profits, and equalization of wealth through social welfare programs and graduated tax measures.

Sovereignty. The characteristic of a nation which renders it truly independent and supreme over its territories and people.

Specie. Money in coin, or hard money.

Status quo. The existing state of affairs.

Status quo ante bellum. Diplomatic term used to describe a peace or armistice based on conditions as they existed before hostilities began.

Tenure. The length or duration of an office held by a public official.

Totalitarianism. A governmental system in which one party or a small group possesses complete control and declares all opposition to be illegal.

Truce. A temporary cessation of hostilities between belligerents which does not provide the groundwork for permanent peace.

Tyrant. One who rules both absolutely (like a dictator) and oppressively and cruelly.

Utopia. An imaginary place or age where everything exists in a perfect state. Any attempt to create a perfect social or political system is utopian.

Visit and Search. The right of a belligerent to stop, board, and search a neutral merchant vessel on the high seas to determine if it might be carrying contraband.

Index